IS ANY SICK AMONG YOU?

(James 5:14)

by

LaDean Griffin

Distributed By:
BI-WORLD PUBLISHERS
P. O. Box 62
Provo, Utah 84601

Dedication

To my mother and father
who inspired me always
to seek after the truth.

PREFACE

Aristotle said, "Dear is Plato, but dearer still is truth." Dear to the world is medical science, and to challenge her scientific findings would be to offend many. Aristotle disagreed with many of Plato's thoughts; nevertheless, he was Plato's devoted student. Many also are the things Aristotle believed which Plato taught that have since been found to be erroneous. However, much of our scientific knowledge can be attributed to their brilliant observations. Their speculations struck an illuminating fire that set men to thinking.

I have been a devoted student of medical history and science; and as Aristotle, who loved and respected those who labored in the cause of truth, I also find much that is promoted and maintained by tradition to be untrue and even detrimental to the health and well-being of society. In challenging medical science, and traditional opinion, I stick my neck out, hoping someone to follow will carry this work out with even more resolute detail and varied observations, studying each herb and its use, and each food which I maintain is for the use of mankind for improvement of health and correction of illness. From a scientific position, my summaries may be superficial. My cruder observations may well be forgiven when it is considered how narrow a circle of experimental equipment I have used to pioneer these thoughts. By the medical profession I am compelled to remain in a position which restricts physical and biological research.

I am not a doctor. I have no degrees of higher learning, only a high school education; my conclusions are drawn from twenty-five years of study and a love of learning. In my opinion, the self-taught person is somewhat discriminated against for no logical reason; most of the great ideas which have changed lives were brought to us by people who did not receive their knowledge from an accredited school, much less a book. Society has even made the discovery of a truth an intolerable burden to those who wish to share these truths with their fellows. Often as we have seen in history, recognition is not granted until the person is long gone from this world. These truths which I sincerely believe, and am going to open to your view, I learned almost twenty-five years ago and have spent these many years in search of the reasons that they are true. Many of my conclusions as to why my beliefs are true may be clouded by the persuasions through books and by the understanding of medical science. If by physical and biological research other truths come to light that can change my views or broaden my understanding of why they are true, I welcome the knowledge. However, the main truths that I wish to express to you, I have already proven to myself without doubt, and I do not excuse myself on this account. Some of the statements I make will be in this category. I have proven these to myself, and many others have proven them also. In these cases I can only say that it works, though I do not know why. I will wait, in the hope that I might find out or that someone will be persuaded to research these ideas and relieve the general atmosphere of suffering and the high cost of dying.

The truth I discovered is that disease can be eliminated and wonderful health maintained when the body is clear of debris and properly fed. I have also found that there can be an almost total cleansing and reconstruction through fasting and semi-fasting foods. Then with the correct foods, beautiful, immaculate health can be gained even in an inherently weak body. I have not always obeyed these truths. I have jumped back and forth, and experimented, always hoping nature would not be so exacting in her laws of health. Still I seemed to be driven by a fierce and constant sense of knowing that I already had the answer. Like algebra problems, I only needed to find out why they were so. As I filled my mind's world with endless debate, having little training for this new pursuit, I was led in many directions — all which brought me safely back to my original conclusions. Testimonies have filled my cup to overflowing, showing me the accuracy of these answers. I have raised six children (the oldest at this writing is 29 years old, the youngest is 10) without the assistance of a physician, except at delivery or in case of accident. However, I did not raise them without the help of Heaven. I lived for two years on fruit and nuts as an experiment. I have never in my life, before or since, been so well. I bore my fourth child during this period, with no pain or anesthetics, and nursed her for one year. She was a beautiful, healthy child, and is now a beautiful, healthy young lady. I became aware at this time that the foods people eat cause their bodies to be either beautiful and healthy or corrupt and inefficient.

As I told of my experiences, I also became aware that few people wanted to know anything that would change their traditional beliefs, much less deprive them of the many dead foods to which they had become accustomed. I could see that somehow, even the threat of being constantly ravaged by pestilence or of being enslaved for extended periods of time by high medical costs did not seem to worry anyone into obedience to nature's laws. Only a desire to know the truth, or perhaps great suffering, can really motivate those of idealistic minds into finding the truth. If you can hear me out, learn by my experience and by my mistakes, there is help for those who suffer, and it is not a utopian dream. These things written are from my own personal experience and observation and are in no way intended to prescribe for anyone, but rather to be informative as to some methods people have used in the art of healing. It is also not my intention to make of this work a specific theological study of any religion, other than Christianity in general. I quote several times from Brigham Young and Joseph Smith and many other great men of the past, only to show their knowledge of these things. I quote, also, the *Doctrine and Covenants* and the *Book of Mormon* because of their interest to me personally. For those persons who are involved in the natural method field, it may be of interest to know what these writers thought. Let us walk together awhile and reason as we go.

The Author

FOREWARD

Voltaire said, "If you wish to converse with me define your terms." Before we begin, I would like to define my terms. When I speak of "drugs" I mean anything made from inorganic sources, except where I speak of the young people taking hard drugs as I realize marijuana is an herb. Many herbs are considered to be drugs. Many herbs are an essential part of the inorganic, man-made drug products on the market. They are a mixture of plant and inorganic chemicals. When they are both, I will call them chemical or drug. When they are entirely chemical, they will be referred to as drug. When they are herbs or plants only, I will call them herbs. All through history, herbs have been called drugs as well as herbs and were, of course, not made of inorganic substances until Paracelsus and others of his time began to introduce inorganic substances (chemicals) into the bodies of men. Do not be confused by the strange concoctions added to the herbs in the apothecary; these will not be referred to as either drug or herb. In this way I will make a definition so you may understand the line that has been drawn between the "Nature doctor" and the medical doctor. When I speak of vitality in reference to healing, I use the term to denote the body's ability to throw off toxic waste.

The Author

CONTENTS

CHAPTER ONE

HERBS TO DRUGS AND BACK TO HERBS

James 5:14-15:

> *"IS ANY SICK AMONG YOU? Let him call for the elders of the church; and let them pray over him, anointing him with oil in the name of the Lord;*
> *"And the prayer of faith shall save the sick, and the Lord shall raise him up; and if he has committed sins, they shall be forgiven him."*

In a store recently, I made the casual remark to a man as he was complaining about world situations, "Maybe it will be better in the next world." Surprised at my comment, he said, "Do you really believe there is a life after death?" As we talked I could see by his attempts to convince me that there is nothing after death, he had had no experience with the principle of faith — other than going about his daily duties. I told him that faith is the key to opening the door to spiritual experiences and that without these experiences he would not know that there is life after death. I told him that signs follow those who believe; faith first, then experiences with heavenly or spiritual things follow. As I left the store I felt truly sorry for the man who had not one witness to his name in behalf of a life hereafter, or that there really is a God. At the age of eight years when I became completely paralyzed with polio, I was given my first glimpse into the infinite power that can heal through faith, as I stood up after three days, completely well. I have since seen many miracles — tuberculosis healed instantly; polio (other than my case), fevers, and pain removed immediately; and new bones put into place. There are many wonderful and beautiful personal experiences I could relate on healing through faith; but since many of them are too sacred to me, and since each person must find his own testimony, I will not relate these at this time. We do not always have sufficient faith to be healed. Nor does God always heal us. Sometimes there are lessons yet to be learned and laws yet to be obeyed.

My intention is to help you tap this vast resource of faith. As Jeremiah 17:5 says,

> "Thus saith the Lord; cursed be the man that trusteth in man, and maketh flesh his arm, and whose heart departeth from the Lord."

Doctrine and Covenants 1:19 reads,

> "The weak things of the world shall come forth and break down the mighty and strong ones, that man should not counsel his fellow men, neither trust in the arm of flesh." ·

According to the Book of Mormon, II Nephi 4:34,

> "O Lord, I have trusted in thee, and I will trust in thee forever. I will not put my trust in the arm of flesh; for I know that cursed is he that putteth his trust in the arm of flesh. Yea, cursed is he that putteth his trust in man or maketh flesh his arm."

Surely today we are cursed with pain, much illness, and high cost of treatment. We have been brainwashed with the thought that we should never do anything for ourselves without consulting a doctor, so that it even takes a great deal of faith to follow the admonition given for those who do not have faith:

D. & C. 42:43

> "And whosoever among you are sick and have not faith to be healed, but believe, shall be nourished with all tenderness, with herbs and mild food, and that not at the hand of an enemy."

It is time we begin to do some thinking for ourselves. It is time we begin to seek more after the spiritual blessings, rather than to reap the cursings spoken of by Jeremiah. Joseph Smith said on Sunday, September 5, 1841:

Documentary History of the Church 4:414

> "I preached to a large congregation at the stand on the

science and practice of medicine, desiring to persuade the
saints to trust in God when sick, and not in the arm of flesh.
And led by faith, and not by medicine or poison; when they
were sick and had called for the elders to pray for them, and
they were not healed, to use herbs and mild food."

Smith further states: D.H.C. 6:183-185

*"I had tried for a number of years to get the minds of the
saints prepared to receive the things of God; but we frequently
see some of them, after suffering all they have for the work of
God, will fly to pieces like glass as soon as anything comes that
is contrary to their traditions. They cannot stand the fire at all.
How many will be able to abide a celestial law, and go through
to receive their exaltation, I am unable to say, as many are
called but few are chosen."*

It is time we begin to come out of the world of materialism and move
into a more spiritual world in preparation for the millenium. We need to
look into the spiritual in all things — plants, animals, ourselves, and
each other. If we are to survive the trials promised by prophecy before
the coming of the Savior, we must find out individually by the spirit just
what makes us tick. We have too long lived with the world of chemicals,
attempting to force chemicals to adapt to our bodies, trying to prove we
are smarter than God. Until we resolve this problem and bring ourselves
into harmony with God's laws of nature, both physical and spiritual, we
will remain in spiritual darkness. We have filled our bodies and our live
plants and animals with chemicals, poisons and drugs and have created
in ourselves a filthiness, a pain, a stink, a death, a confusion of mind, a
nervousness, and a stress unbearable. We run to and fro trying to find
peace and health. We burden ourselves with more stress to earn the
money to pay high medical costs and the high cost of death. We burden
ourselves with the acquisition of worldly things. Vapors of smoke rise
from our cities to further pollute our bodies and our lungs, all to make
sacrifice to the God of money. We chop down our orchards and fill the
spaces with "house upon house and city upon city." On our holidays
and Sabbaths, we rush from this insanity to the beaches or mountains to
find a little peace to draw a charge again on our low body battery, only to
find everyone else is there struggling for a spot. We have filled mother
earth's life water arteries in her old age with pollution and waste. With
all the bad blood of generations and being the children of an old mother
earth, whose strength and vigor are weakened, we add insult to the earth
and do hurt to her and to ourselves, with all the sophistication and
self-assurance of an insane man who thinks he is Napoleon.

13

It is time we begin to look to the things God has created to heal and feed our bodies. It is time we begin to analyze what we have in the vegetation surrounding us and stop the senseless attempt to create health and life in a test tube. It is time we free ourselves from the death grip of science and worldly things to look to the spirit of man. It is time to give our children health and strength, peace and happiness, the kind that can only be given through healthy bodies and pure spirits.

As II Nephi 28:20 reads;

"For behold, at that day shall he rage in the hearts of the children of men, and stir them up to anger against that which is good."

The children of our generation have been easy targets for this rage of Satan, with their sickly bodies and poor vibrations, in a world filled with greed and chemical life. Even when some of these children have turned from the worldly things, without sufficient spiritual knowledge and understanding, Satan could set another snare in their path.

Zola said of Ceyanne,

"I remember, however, after receiving one of his missives from the providence, having said to him, 'I like these strange thoughts of yours, like young Bohemians with their bizarre glances, their dirty feet, and their heads in flowers.' But I could not help adding, 'Our sovereign master of the public is more difficult to satisfy. It does not care a snap for princesses dressed in rags. To find grace in its eyes we must not only say something but we must say it well.' "

History has shown us that when a nation becomes ripe in iniquity and is ready to fall, the young, seeking a place of refuge from the chaos and finding no peace in the religions of the day, turn to the mystical religions of the east. Oriental apathy and resignation found ready soil in a despondent and decadent Greece. Stoic philosophies by Zeno, 310 B.C., and epicureanism were Oriental infiltrations into Greek life and thought. Alexander, a student tutored by Aristotle in his hour of triumph, found himself conquered by the soul of the east. The flower children are not new to the world of history. Often, in a decaying society, as the young have sought escape, Satan has used these same tools to ensnare them. He entices them to turn to the theosophic and mystical through self-development and concentration; in so doing, he gives them powers they know nothing about, powers they think are rewards for righteousness or concentration, while he used them during their deep sense of mortal preoccupation into the complete relinquishment of responsibility toward their fellowmen, families, friends, and to a place where they give all homage to their God, Satan. The *Bhagavad Gita* says, led "He who thinks constantly thinketh upon Me, not thinking ever of them another, of him I am easily reached."

What a contrast from Christ's statements:

Matthew 25:40

> "Inasmuch as ye have done it unto one of the least of these my brethren, ye have done it unto me."

And;

John 15:13

> "Greater love hath no man than this, that a man lay down his life for his friends."

Yes, in hope of peace, some of the young have strayed from all the sound principles of real love for a counterfeit of self-love. They gradually turn from what began with the thought of love to a quiet, self-imposed serenity which apathetically excludes all pain and suffering of their fellowmen, families, or friends. Then they will usually turn to more self-imposed restrictions of diet and sex, often excluding sex entirely, becoming celibate. Where this is too difficult and the roots of responsibility have been completely severed, they turn to homosexuality or free love without responsibility to mother or child. We see in China and India the plight of mother and children in a world where men have forsaken their responsibility, to make a place only for serenity under all circumstances. What a delusion, living constantly ravished by pestilence, famine, and squalor, holding the thought that if they can take it on the chin long enough, they will reach the perfection of nirvana where they will be suddenly absolved into God, losing their identity, becoming nothing and nobody. Such a reward for a life of pain and suffering. Yes, there are many roads to hell besides the obvious no-good, mean-type person, many that have been paved with self-sacrifice and seeming righteousness. Satan knows them all and uses them best in an establishment tottering and weakened from within — sickly bodies made so by perverted tastes and unscrupulous advertising, wicked men sacrificing the younger generation to the God of money — fertile ground for the young to be confused and willing to trade a drug trip (real living, man!)

a real spiritual experience, to mistake love for lust, to trade indulgence for sickness and death, or to trade self-sacrifice for an eternal prize of nothingness, to trade one of life's most rewarding experiences, work, for play.

Michelangelo said,

> "Nothing makes the soul so pure, so religious, as the endeavor to create something perfect; for God is perfection, and whoever strives for it, strives for something that is Godlike. True painting is only an image of God's perfection, a shadow of the pencil with which he paints, a melody, a striving after harmony."

To trade the experience and wisdom of good parents for a legacy of corruption and degradation, to throw down all established rules, good or bad, so they can begin the next decade with no rules at all, to throw out all the timeless music and art which has touched the heartstrings of mankind for generations, as people have stood in awe, brought to tears of joy by their beauty, and trade this for the bizarre, loud rhythm of passion and torment is a pathetic display of the chain of reasoning being infiltered into the minds of our youth. Tolstoy said, "Every Charlatan artist when he invents a new fad in art, also trots out a private definition of his own to justify that fad," Goethe said, "The chord that wakes a kindred heart tone, must first be tuned and vibrate in your own."

Yes, Satan is doing his utmost to confuse, degrade and despoil the young. While he tries to destroy the young, he has not forgotten the middle aged or the old. With his drugs of destruction, he sweeps from under heaven all who fall under their spell.

Oliver Wendell Holmes made a statement in 1862, almost prophetic of the Twentieth Century:

> "What ever elements nature does not introduce into vegetables, the natural food of all animal life, directly of herbivorous, indirectly of carnivorous animals – are to be regarded with suspicion. The disgrace of medicine has been a colossal system of self-deception, in obedience to which mines have been emptied of their cankering minerals, the vegetable kingdom robbed of its noxious growths, the entrails of animals taxed for their impurities, the poison bags of reptiles drained of their venom, and all the inconceivable abominations thus obtained, thrust down the throats of human beings suffering

from some fault of organization, nourishment or vital stimulation."

Mr. Holmes wrote his entire medical essay against the chemical drug therapy moving in on the medical scene of his day. He was very much against the drug quacks who were taking over the care of the sick. I wonder what he would think of the death-grip medical chemical-therapy has on the people of the earth today. Let's go back to the beginning and analyze what has happened in the history of medicine to see how it has affected our lives and how the pendulum has swung from herbal medicines to drugs, and how it is now on the swing back to natural herbs. The study of drugs has brought us somewhat out of the darkness of the superstition which added a spider's leg or a cat's tooth to the herbs in the apothecary jar, has taught us to analyze each element and identify it singly, yet has led us into an even deeper abyss of drug superstition.

The oldest records we have in medicine, we find in Egypt and Babylon. Fortunately for us, the Egyptians believed in life after death where embalming was practiced between 4,000 B.C. and A.D. 600. Two excellent papyrus books which aid us in understanding the medicine practice at that time were uncovered at Thebes, The Edwin Smith papyrus (1862) and the Eber papyrus (1872).

EB. 106 mentions a donkey head or leg.
EB. 108 pig's tooth in a bandage.
EB. 580 an ass's tooth dissolved in water.

We find many of the names of herbs strange to us today, while many of them remain the same. Some names have been changed while the herb is still known. Licorice, for instance, was called Scythian root and was placed in the tombs of Egypt. I believe that the names of the herbs above have brought the actual pig's tooth to the apothecary by taking literally from ancient writings what I feel sure was the name of an herb: we would not put a fox's glove in the medicine, or a snapdragon. When a remedy called for the tooth of the God Thot, I feel it was possibly representing a secret or popular name. There was much that was secret among the physicians and always has been, up until our day. This could have been their medical lingo just as we have a secret medical language today. Many filthy articles were added later in history to the herbs in the apothecary, probably because of taking the ancient name of the herb literally. These people were not stupid, and they certainly healed the sick. The physicians were of the clergy, priests and scribes. Their temples were beautifully clean and the priests dressed in white. It may have been only for the sake of beauty; we do not know if they understood sanitation principles. If they did, these things were not passed on to succeeding generations. Babylon and Assyria also had their physicians who again were priests, and much of their work consisted of incantations and faith healing. They kept their God benevolent by human sacrifice when they felt he was offended. They charged a fee for services, and if they failed in surgery, they had their hands cut off. It took great courage to be either physician or patient. If a doctor could do three successful surgeries on an infidel (not of his nation) he was allowed to practice.

Moses was the next important public health leader. We read in Leviticus and Deutoronomy the laws and code of health practiced by Ancient Israel. A practice of the laws of sanitation was strictly enforced. Levite priests were keenly aware of direct transmission of disease from one individual to another. Directions were given for isolation of the people infected. Hygiene and preventive medicine were a part of their way of life. Sickness was considered a sin, because they realized that as long as they did the things they were commanded, they stayed well. Sickness, thought of as the result of sin, has been part of the theories of almost all peoples at all times of the world's existence; but Israel's concept of it was entirely different from that of most other religions. Their belief in correct diet and strict obedience did bring with it the rewards of health and, furthermore, was backed up by the word of the Lord:

Exodus 15:26

"I will put none of these diseases upon thee, which I have brought upon the Egyptians, for I am the Lord that healeth thee."

The Talmud contains more precise medical knowledge even than the Old Testament. Much of it is based upon superstition, and some on sound principles:

Talmud p shab 4b:

"There is a saying in Babylon that hot bread has fever by its side."

In an attempt to make a commentary on the law of Moses, the old Rabbis, mixing superstition with the law, made it as complicated at times as the medical science of today, and with about as many errors.

The Greeks were next in the limelight on the medical stage. They were craftsmen, traveling from place to place selling their services, much like a traveling salesman. If they were fortunate or a better physician, they were retained annually by a family, or by many families; people had their own doctor, much like they do today. Homer's *Iliad* and the *Odyssey* give us much information about the treatments. Aesculapius temple centers of faith healing existed at this time. They were much like the health resorts of today — places of refuge from the world. With quiet sleep, it was thought by faith that when you awakened you would be healed. With soft music, priest incantations and a beautiful atmosphere — people did recover. Of course we know how it worked; getting away to some quiet beautiful place is usually always therapeutic. Hippocrates, 400 B.C., had no connection with these temple hospitals. In fact, he was much against them. He tried to take medicine to a position which completely excluded sin demons and gods as the cause of disease, trying to find the answers entirely in natural causes, away from any superstition of faith healings. His aim was to take medical practice away from the clergy. He is considered the father of modern medicine, but many of his ideas are far removed from medical practices of today. He wrote, "Your food should be your medicine, and your medicine your food." Modern medicine somehow lost track of the food idea in the illusion of chemical therapy. The one similarity we recognize with medical practice today is the complete disregard for anything supernatural — I am speaking generally, not individually.

19

When a science or a people become so smug and sophisticated as to leave God out, the young so often begin to find spiritual experiences with the occult. Hippocrates wrote 70 books on medicine. His favorite medicine, it may interest you to know, was honey — and vinegar and honey for pain. He said, "Common sense is the rarest of all commodities." Hippocrates has been much respected over the years. His concept that nature is the great healer, and that it is our duty to assist and not to hinder her in her task, has persisted for 800 years. Our European medicine, which dates from the Renaissance, has not lasted that long; and from the looks of things, we are in need of a change. Mr. and Mrs. Lay Public, who are getting fed up with the high cost of medicine and are becoming more ill with the use of chemical drugs, are turning more and more interest to nature and her methods. The youngsters who have gone off into the drug kick and have realized that it was killing them found their own way back to vitamin C, brown rice and herbs. They did not go to the medical doctor because they knew that all he had to offer them was more drugs. Some of the wiser ones have gone to organic gardening, organic stores, herbs and organic restaurants. Because of the stress caused by the drugs, they have had to find a spirituality to quiet and ease the pain of a tortured nervous system. Because they, at this point, cannot cope with the rat race or with the strain of lifting someone else when they themselves are at the bottom of the barrel, the selfish religions of the east quiet them and give them rest. Let's hope that when their souls are rested from the turmoil of drugs they will be able to find their way back to Christ's method of lifting and helping, sharing, and loving others equally with themselves. The sick, for a time, may have to be selfish: the well can afford to be generous. The problem is trying to stay well in the society in which we live. The problem also is that some young people may never loosen themselves from the selfish religions of Satan. However, some of these people are finding a way back to Christianity which is based on vitality, vibrantly beautiful health, real love and peace. Christianity is a moving, active, going concern, carrying a beautiful aura of inner peace with it that lifts and helps wherever it goes — not a stagnant, sit-on-a cushion, selfish-type religion which in its selfishness misses most of the wonder and beauty of life, love and people.

PERFECTION, in my opinion, is to find a serenity and peace of soul and still love deeply enough to be involved in the pain and sorrow of others. If love of hurt for others destroys, perfection flees. Love must always lift and help; there is no room in love or perfection for self-pity. Self-pity and grief are sisters. You cannot lift another from his sinking boat if you are in the boat with him. Love must stay out enough to be on steady ground, but close enough to reach the outstretched hand.

Turning back to the next character in the history of medicine, Aristotle explored man and beast and did much for the advancement of modern biology.

When the Romans began their rule of the world, Caesar, 46 B.C., welcomed the Greek physician, developed a public hygiene, and taxed the people to pay for it. Greek doctors lived tax free with an annual salary from the government or from private citizens. If they were born free, they were awarded Roman citizenship. If they were exceptionally good at their profession, they were reserved by the rich or important and were paid as much as $10,000 for an operation or cure. Their cures were herbs and food.

The dashing, handsome, dynamic, egotistical and dogmatic personality of Galen arrives on the stage of history approximately A. D. 138, and he is considered to be the father of experimental physiology. He wrote 400 books; lectured on animals and animal dissection and discovered there was blood in the veins rather than air, as was previously thought; proved that the ebb and flow movement of blood was brought about by the pumping action of the heart; but failed to learn exactly how the body functioned. Developing his own theories (and some of them made a very accurate measure of how sick a person was) he could also determine accurately the rate of recovery. He taught about four humors — blood, phlegm, yellow bile and black bile. He considered that when these were out of balance or when any one of them was in excess, it meant a given problem. He used herbs, food fasting, baths, fresh air, poultices, purgatives and diuretics accordingly. The various herbs he used were cooling, some heating and some moistening. Galen apparently had a great understanding of the use of herbs and how to put them in combination. He seemd to have known the varying degrees of effectiveness each herb and how to put it into formula to complement the other. This was truly remarkable without the knowledge of the chemistry we have today which allows us to identify each given factor. If this kind of study could only be done today on herbs, rather than on chemicals, we might learn some of the secrets he knew.

His methods for healing the sick must have had some measure of success as his theories persisted long into the Eighteenth Century. Even the practice of blood letting (trephining) for plethora or an excess of blood, considered at that time to be the most common cause of disease, helped many people with either too much pressure or too much toxic waste in the blood. In some instances in history, the letting of blood was associated with superstition that it released the demons causing the illness. Many of the purification ideas, baths and fasts, were associated with sin being the cause of illness, making it necessary to offer sacrifice to appease their Gods. All in all, however, viewing the good that Galen did, it is a sorry thing that when some of his practices were proven wrong, all of the rest were discarded. A great deal of Hippocrates' and Galen's methods were just common sense. As Hippocrates said, "Common sense is the rarest of all commodities." Some of their procedures to remove waste or to rebuild with food are just as true today as they were then.

You will remember Luke the physician who always traveled with the Apostle Paul. It is thought that Paul had some kind of physical weakness for which he was in constant need of a physician. Luke was of the Greek school. As we move on into the Middle Ages and the church again dominates the people under Christianity and the popes, the church prescribes faith, as Christ was the Great Healer. Greek medicine takes a back seat with a marked disrespect, as Christians were excommunicated from the church if they either studied the Galen method or had the help of a Greek physician, as Greek medicine was considered a pagan art. Many truths in medicine were overcome by the mental stagnation of the Middle Ages. The monks began to run the hospitals where again faith healing was the thing of the day. Only comfort and sympathy were the lot of the sick who sought escape from pain and death. As the Greeks' radiance and power deteriorated sharply, the search for truth in medicine swung across the sea to the Moslems and Jews.

Avicenna was the great man of the day. At 20 years of age he was considered the most learned man in the world. His medical books were used for over 600 years and are still occasionally used in the Orient. He wrote 68 books on philosophy and theology, 11 books on anatomy and science, 16 on medicine and four on poetry. He became the first Arabian druggist with the first drugstore. Many pilgrimages are still made to his tomb. Moslem rule was benevolent and tolerant at this period. It is unfortunate for us that later periods of history became so intolerant as to burn many of the works of the great thinkers. If all the books written on medicine had managed to survive the prejudices of political powers of succeeding generations, what an excellent work we could have from which to draw. Like much of the lost word of God, the history of medicine is greatly depleted when it gets down to us because a few bigoted rulers or peoples thought they alone had an edge on the truth, so they burned anything contradictory to their beliefs. Much of our scholarly modern world has narrowed into this same kind of pinched thinking on the grounds that anything written, dated later than yesterday, is obsolete.

As a student of Avicenna's work and the law of Moses around 1135, Moses Maimonides stands out in history at this period as one of the great physicians, son of a Rabbi, student of the Mosiac Law, and scholar. Spain at the time became the center of world learning until the Inquisition broke down all quests for knowledge, absolving all scholarly pursuits into the ferociously solemn and narrow ideology of the church. Great scholars among the Jews were burned at the stake until, finally, the people became sickened by the atrocities. The remainder were expelled from the country, and among them was Maimonides, His great works to the Jews were the *Guide to the Perplexed* and the *Mishna Torah*. He was also author of the 13 articles of faith the Jews use today. With his great knowledge it was natural that he whould become a physician. Living in Alexandria, he became physician to Saladin. Since he wrote his books in Arabic, a young Jew wrote to him, wishing to solicit his help in the translation of his books to the Hebrew language. His answer may be of interest, showing his dedication as a physician, also his ability to be in such demand:

"Now God knows that in order to write this to you I have escaped to a secluded spot, where people would not think to find me, sometimes leaning for support against the wall, sometimes lying down on account of my excessive weakness, for I have grown old and feeble.

"With regard to your wish to come here to me, I cannot but say how greatly your visit would delight me, for I truly long to commune with you, and would anticipate our meeting with even greater joy than you. Yet I must advise you not to expose

yourself to the perils of the voyage, for beyond seeing me, and my doing all I could to honor you, you would not derive any advantage from your visit. Do not expect to be able to confer with me on any scientific subject, for even one hour either by day or by night, for the following is my daily occupation. I dwell at Misr (Fostat) and the Sultan resides at Kahira (Cairo); these two places are two Sabbath days journey (about one mile and a half) distant from each other. My duties to the Sultan are very heavy. I am obliged to visit him every day, early in the morning; and when he or any of his children, or any of the inmates of his harem, are indisposed, I dare not quit Kahira, but must stay during the greater part of the day in the palace. It also frequently happens that one or two of the royal officers fall sick, and I must attend to their healing.

"Hence, as a rule, I repair to Kahira very early in the day, and if nothing unusual happens, I do not return to Misr until the afternoon. Then I am almost dying with hunger. I find the antechamber filled with people, both Jews and Gentiles, nobles and common people, judges and bailiffs, friends and foes – mixed multitude, who await the time of my return.

"I dismount from my animal, wash my hands, go forth to my patients, and entreat them to bear with me while I partake of some slight refreshment, the only meal I take in the twenty-four hours. Then I attend to my patients, writing prescriptions for their various ailments. Patients go in and out until night-fall, and sometimes even, I solemnly assure you, until two hours and more in the night, I converse and prescribe for them while lying down from sheer fatigue, and when night falls I am exhausted that I can scarcely speak.

"In consequence of this, no Israelite can have any private interview with me except on the Sabbath. On this day the whole congregation, or at least the majority of the members, come to me after the morning service, when I instruct them as to their proceedings during the whole week; we study together a little until noon, when they depart. Some of them return, and read with me after the afternoon service until evening prayers. In this manner I spend that day. I have here related to you only a part of what you would see if you were to visit me. Now, when you have completed for our brethren the translation you have commenced, I beg that you will come to me but not with the *hope of deriving any advantage from your visit as regards your studies; for my time is, as I have shown you, excessively occupied.''*

His treatises on various medical subjects are available in libraries today. You may be interested in some of the things he taught which are just as true today as they were when he wrote them. If the Jews of today are to spare themselves and manage to escape the impending disasters ahead, they must turn back, in my opinion, to the medical teachings of Moses and old Rabbis of the Talmud, back to the old sage physicians like Moses Maimonides; they must incorporate some of these wonderful old truths into the modern technology which is making of them a great nation. In order to win the battles against the nations who want to wipe them off the map, they will have to be stronger physically, mentally and spiritually than their enemies. As I see it, they must turn from the chemical sprays and fertilizers on their food to natural and organic methods. Bringing back the old-fashioned herbs, making them a part of their new-found wisdom, then searching for better ideas, they will find the correct medicine for the infirmities of their humanity — ridding themselves and their nation of the demons responsible for producing the illness we see so prevalent today. They will see then the necessity of feeding their nation of young sabras on nutritionally sound food and will leave the drug peddler to peddle his wares elsewhere.

Doctors today sophisticatedly study symptoms and reactions to drugs but have missed the causes and, therefore, in some respects do not know as much of the art of healing as the Great Physicians of the past. They seem to be too busy with drug experiments to find the real cause of illness. They seem to live on the premise that 80 per cent of the time the body will heal itself no matter what you do.

During the Arab rule of medicine, Christians were forbidden to go to a Moslem or Jewish physician on pain of excommunication. The law was not strictly enforced, as they were helping too many people. Much like the nature doctor versus the medical doctor today, the struggle has been very uncomfortable, but too many people are getting better by natural methods for it to be shut away in a corner.

In the late Middle Ages medicine moves again to the west to the Salerno school. Laws were enacted prohibiting the clergy from taking part in surgery.

The Renaissance brought with it artists to spearhead medical advances through Michelangelo, Dürer and da Vinci in the study of anatomy; they dissected the bodies of prisoners to discover the structure of muscles, so as to paint and draw more perfectly. With the Renaissance came also the quest for knowledge, culture and beauty.

In 1490-1541 Paracelsus, a Swiss doctor, pioneered applications of chemistry to medicine, through alchemy. He questioned some old values and re-examined some new ones:

> *"It is not title and eloquence, nor the knowledge of language, nor the reading of books, however ornamental, that are the requirements of a physician, but the deepest knowledge of things themselves and of nature's secrets, and this knowledge outweighs all else."*

He also said,

> *"The patient must not be out of the physician's mind day and night. He must put his whole power of reasoning and his judgment deliberately in the service of his patient."*

This would be difficult in our day of detached specialization.

> *"The best of our popular physicians are the ones who do the least harm. But unfortunately some poison their patients with mercury, and others purge or bleed them to death. There are some who have learned so much that their learning has driven out all common sense; and there are others who care a great deal more for their own profit than for the health of their patients – a physician should be the servant of Nature, not his enemy; he should be able to guide and direct her in her struggle for life, and not throw by his unreasonable influences fresh obstacles in the way of recovery."*

25

He further said,

> *"If you are to be a true physician, you must be able to do your own thinking and not merely enjoy the thoughts of others."*

You see, he wrote many good things, and he had the adventuresome attitude of a free thinker. He made many interesting and fresh clinical observations, but he seems to be the one who sat at the helm as we have drifted off into the chemical world of drugs. Writing as he did about nature, I have a feeling he would not appreciate taking the credit for being the father of chemical therapy. It seems we have not come too far from the old ideas about alchemy, when doctors today are giving shots of gold for arthritis. Paracelsus was the first to point out the relationship between goiter and cretinism. His was the first modern theory of metabolism, he was the first to make tincture of opium, and he was the first to introduce inorganic materials into the body.

Paré, in 1545, was the great surgeon. Surgeons during this period were barbers. The physicians were the teachers and scholars, and it was beneath their dignity to soil their hands with surgery. It was a sort of caste system; barber or physician went from father to son. Paré became an especially talented barber surgeon on the battlefield with the French army; later he was surgeon to Henry II and to three succeeding kings. He wrote an interesting little manual, now a medical classic on the treatment of wounds. In the War of 1552 he proved that ligature of the artery was preferable to cauterization to check bleeding in amputations. During his time, boiling oil was used to cauterize wounds. One night Paré ran out of oil to cauterize, so he used some herbs on those men still untreated with hot oil. Going to bed he worried all night that the uncauterized men would be dead in the morning. Upon checking them in the morning he found them much better off than those cauterized — no swelling, no inflammation and no pain. Realizing this Paré wrote his now classic manual. In his writings, like Hippocrates, he always protested the use of remedies which harmed the patient and in this way interfered with nature's healing processes.

The Seventeenth Century began with the rise of democracy, and the old class caste system went with it. Anyone could become a doctor. This was the age of measurement. Cinchona bark was discovered to cure the fevers of malaria. The microscope came on the scene, bringing with it a whole new perspective of all the little creatures of man's environment he had known nothing about. Suddenly these factors were in everything, all around him. Blood transfusion became possible. Surgeons operated on cancer. It was the age of the mad *poison-mixers* of history.

With the dawn of the Eighteenth Century, the age of reason began. Charity was born again; as it gained momentum, neglected little ones were cared for. There began prison reforms. Stephen Hales, in 1677-1761 an English clergyman, developed the first blood pressure gauge. Doctors carried a golden cane filled with herbs, and the surgeon became a gentleman. Withering discovered foxglove (digitalis). In 1796 Jenner discovered the difference between diptheria typhus and typhoid and discovered that vaccination really worked. Doctors during this period were well paid. The midwife knew more about delivery than the doctor, as propriety kept all the secrets between us girls. With the discovery of bacteria, and since Andrias Vesalius in 1543 had already undermined Galen with his beautiful drawings of human anatomy, we see Galen's reign ending. Because he had been wrong about anatomy, it was assumed, with the sight of bacteria's more tangible evidence, that all disease was caused from outside the body from the tiny bugs viewed under the microscope. It is sad that all of Galen's teachings were so disastrously ignored at this time in history. Man seems to have a strange tendency to reject experience and to accept one newfound truth as the living end to all truth. This time medical science missed the main truth and went off in a stumbling manner.

In 1858 Virchow gave his cellular pathology to the world, showing the world how the increase in the number of white blood corpuscles takes place at the onset of an infection. Metschnikoff, 1916, carried on the error, showing how certain types of white corpuscles repelled the body's invasions by hostile organisms; another neutralized the poisons liberated by invading germs; a third, the phagocyte, engulfed and digested the organisms themselves. Strengthening Virchow's theories, starting happily on their way,emerged the erroneous story we have all heard in school about the white corpuscle soldiers who battle to protect us from invaders.

Then began the age of specialism in surgery, orthopedics, dermatology, etc., each running on his own little track, not realizing that there is but one disease. However, much has been learned as a result of the specialist.

To add to the pride of science, ignited by arrogance and boastful rhetoric, a new language began to take shape, a language which would leave the lay person in complete ignorance as to what was wrong with his body, thus strengthening the power of the physician over his fellowmen. The doctor's refusal to share his knowledge in common language could place him in the position, if you thought about it enough, of not knowing all he would like you to think he knows. One great stepping stone to the doctors' pillar of power over humanity lay in the discovery of ether: an operation could be performed with blissful insensibility not known until this time. Many opiates and pain killers had been known and used in the past, but not until the discovery of ether and all succeeding anaesthetics have the use of pain killers been used by all medical doctors. They learned enough about it to remove fear of overdose, which was the reason many pain killers of the past were abandoned at different periods in history. The use of and the knowledge of pain killers and anaesthetics have been selfishly guarded and kept only among the medical doctors and dentists, leaving the nature doctor unable to use any of them. This has placed the nature doctor, by public demand for the pain killer, on the outside, a "quack."

Over the past fifty years, with the help of advertizing, radio and TV shows, the doctor has been raised almost to the place of a God in the public eye. Surgery has increased in knowledge of how to repair and remove parts of the body. This has helped establish the doctors' power. Some things that preceeded surgical knowledge were the quiet measures reinforcing medical dominance, but what came after by way of successful operations in many cases inspired genuine belief that the physician had finally arrived at the place of all knowledge. It is not my intention to discredit a skillful surgeon, as I have the utmost respect for skill. However, I believe man will look back on this era of blood and butchery with horror and pity for the souls who layed their bodies on the sacrificial surgical altars, supposing this was the highest development of science and man. This is the great strength of power on the medical pedestal; but because the doctor, with his drugs, surgery and pain killers is not solving the problems of chronic disease, his position is tottering, and thinking people everywhere are beginning to wonder what he really knows. People are beginning to ask the question that always accompanies progress: Isn't there an easier and better way? The search for alternative solutions has begun.

Going back to the beginning of the Nineteenth Century, and with anaesthetics to allow human guinea pig research, many questions not previously answered have come to light. Many lights of truth from the past were darkened by the sophistication of so-called modern science. With Lister's antiseptic carbolic acid went the last tie to the Galen theory that sickness came from within. Psychology and psychiatry came on the scene; Plato had studied human behavior but in the Nineteenth Century, the first laboratory was set up in Germany to study the mind's reactions to given situations. Sigmund Freud opened the world of the subconscious mind. Pasteur, 1895, in an attempt to save the wine crop, learned how to preserve milk. We now have many milk products available with not much food value. He discovered a cure of rabies and more about vaccination immunization. It appears that the old beliefs that ascribe disease to evil spirits, mists in the air, still persist in the germ theory.

Antoine Beauchamp's teachings were really the beginning of Pasteur's laboratory studies of fermentation. To quote Beauchamps,

"Disease is born of us and in us and that is as it should be, because the life of man, and of every other creature is no more delivered over to chance than the course of the stars. Life would be delivered over to chance if it depended upon primitive microbic germs created for destructive purposes."

Beauchamp's views were shared by Rudolf Virchow:

"If I could live my life over again I would devote it to proving that germs seek their natural habitat, diseased tissue, rather than being the cause of the diseased tissue."

Because Pasteur was a chemist working in a laboratory, rather than a physician with experience at the bedside, he missed the real truth that an analytical mind like his could have seen in a moment — that a normal, healthy, well-nourished man has a natural immunity to germs. Fruits, vegetables, man and animal have this immunity as long as they are properly nourished or are without the flaw of inherent weakness. The action of germs comes only secondary and only invade when the living organism is perverted. At the vulnerable point, the bacteriological fermentation starts; microbes or bacteria are scavengers and are only found in decaying cells, waste matter, always attempting to bring us back to dust.

Koch began to grow bacteria and learned to identify tuberculosis. The antiseptic white clean hospital came into its own; nurses became a tender, dignifying, graceful part of the clean, white environment. The squalor and repellent painful atmosphere which had been strongly linked to the healing profession was scrubbing its hands and floors. The hospital began to be a place of refuge from pain, a place to rest where every need was met, a place to take a loved one in pain when you did not know what to do for him.

Child care and child psychology became the interest of the day. Since tenderness in the care of the sick was becoming a part of society, more tenderness was diverted towards the children. With the dawn of psychology it was decided that maybe there was more to little Johnny's problem than anything physical: "Don't spank him, you may give him a complex." The wayward independence and rebellion of youth today began a gradual process as the discipline of parents became steadily and increasingly undermined by the psycologists' theories. Many good things have also come from the study of psychology, however.

Early in the Twentieth Century man almost found a way to combine the truths learned in surgery with Hippocrates' ideas about food for medicine: pursuing the common aim of health for everyone, all health-minded poople ecstatically celebrated the convincing study of the vitamin value in food. Today, only the nature people cling to the old vitamin theory. For the most part, the medical doctor has been frustrated as the chemist began to make the vitamin from synthetics, with the result that they did not work only to stimulate, gradually leaving the doctor disenchanted for lack of a given result to help his patient. He then began to tell them the only way to get vitamins was from their food, and before long he hardly believed in vitamins in food.

With the discovery of insulin by Best and Banting in 1921 and the relief from the fear of diabetes, man moved even more quickly into chemical therapy. The conflict sharpened between natural methods and drugs. The roads in the health circles divided with an accumulated bitterness as each went his separate way. Because the medical people had the power of release from pain, they could rule, and did. The medical hospitals and medical schools increased. The secret language vocabulary grew. Large chemical companies grew in strength and power.

Research continued on all chemical levels until only the drug salesman really could tell the doctor what was new on the market. With the doctor's busy practice, he depended more and more on the drug salesman. The drug industry began to be big business, really big business, and its stranglehold tightened around the throats of Mr. and Mrs. Public. When the drug salesman arrived at the doctor's office, everyone waited while he gave the doctor samples and literature about new and wonderful research to assure the survival of mankind through drugs. Even the doctor began to be the slave of the drug companies. If he believed anything about natural methods, he dared not use it or speak of it lest he be excommunicated from the use of the medical hospital and his only means of support.

The interesting thing about drugs is that there are only a few main drugs, like the keys on a piano, the same keys being repeated over and over. What you buy when you have a prescription filled is a brand name, usually a big long name, another part of the medical secret lingo designed to help keep friend doctor on his pedestal. You think, "Wow, he knows so much." Have you ever been to the doctor and had him say, "There is a new drug that has been researched that may be able to help you." He hands you a small bottle and says, "Try this and let me know how it works." You think he is really great; you didn't even have to pay for a prescription — how nice. You may take it home and become worse, so you call him and tell him how violently you reacted to it, so he says reassuringly, "Discontinue it and come in and we will try something else." When the samples are left by the drug salesman and the folders about the drug are read, you, Mr. and Mrs. Public, become the guinea pig; and when the doctor finds one that works on most people, it becomes one of those big names he frequently prescribes.

With World War II came the antibiotics, followed by the disappointment of the use of sulfa, the wonder drug. With the continual use of drugs, and more and more additives and preservatives added to the foods, cancer was on the up and up, and also heart disease. With only penicillin and surgery to strengthen their position and when the medical practice had no more to offer in the way of a spectacular new discovery, they sought out the African witch doctor and the medicine man and made some startling discoveries which could have been useful; but for the sake of money, they made cortisone synthetically, and it has become a "dud" like sulfa.

The discovery of the hormone balance has been a great breakthrough if man could only figure out a way to work with nature and not against her. With the ever-increasing supreme mental tension of a fast-moving society, with less and less true nourishment, and with more and more chemicals illing peoples' bodies, no one really had the time to let nature clean and clear the waste from his body. With everyone getting weaker and sicker, the protein theory came on the scene with a bang. Heavy protein completely stops the process of elimination, so the minute your body becomes weak as the process of elimination starts to cleanse, you eat a heavy protein — or the popular "vogue" of today, take a protein drink — and you are immediately stronger. You justify all the protein advertising and agree wholeheartedly with the learned men of science who tell you that protein builds your body.

With the discovery of all the major hormone drugs came the hallucinogenics, the barbituates and amphetamines. With the use of heavy narcotic drugs by a larger percentage of young people than ever before in history, along with the use of the drugs, came an ideology; and ideologies arouse deep emotion and strong and sometimes strange loyalties. II Timothy 3:5

> "This know also, that in the last days perilous times shall come. For men shall be lovers of their own selves, covetous, boasters, proud, blasphemers, disobedient to parents, unthankful, unholy, without natural affection, trucebreakers, false accusers, incontinent, fierce, despisers of those that are

31

good, traitors, heady, highminded, lovers of pleasures more than lovers of God; having a form of godliness, but denying the power thereof; from such turn away."

With the use of anaesthetics the midwife's eminent sovereignty over the birth of children was relinquished to the man with the power to relieve the pain. With growing completeness, women have become rigidly subservient to the system. There have been a few brave souls in the last few years who have sought to have their babies the natural way without anaesthetics. Some have been richly rewarded for their efforts and have proven, at least to themselves, that when Eve was told that she would bring forth children in sorrow that it did not necessarily mean physical pain.

It has proven what Brigham Young so prophetically said in his *Journal of Discourses*, 15, page 225,

"Would you want doctors? Yes, to set bones. We should want a good surgeon for that, or to cut off a limb. But do you want doctors? For not much of anything else, let me tell you, only the traditions of the people lead them to think so; and here is a growing evil in our midst. It will be so in a little time that not a woman in all Israel will dare to have a baby unless she can have a doctor by her. I will tell you what to do, you ladies, when you find you are due to have an increase, go off into some country where you can not call for a doctor, and see if you can keep it. I guess you will have it, and I guess it will be all right too."

As a result of the controlled system for the birth of children, many things have been learned which were not known in past times. Women have been lifted (at least until she gives up all rights to the privileges of womanhood) to a remarkably high place in the western world. Childbirth has so often in history been looked upon with the reproach of the unclean, and is still considered so in many places in the world today. It may sound, from my comments, that I am against all medical doctors. May I say that I am not. There are many times when surgery and the knowledge that has been gained by it has been a great blessing to accident victims. There are times when there is no other course but surgery. Surely, who am I to place all doctors into one imcompetent lump. There are many devoted, kindly men who give of themselves continually. Not meaning any discredit to them, often the only sympathy and consolation a woman could find in delivery was given by her doctor, which of course has also strengthened his position. Having someone to tell your troubles to is always a comfort, even if you have to pay him to listen. We all need someone at these times of pain and sorrow. This of course causes the attachment to grow between doctor and patient. It looks like in most cases we have lost the tenderness and devotion of the old country doctor, even though the propaganda on the latest doctor TV shows would try to convince us otherwise. There are also many medical men who have pioneered and have been condemned by their own because they discovered truth and wrote on natural methods. If there were only some way for the knowledge and truth from both sides to merge, to bless mankind.

In many ways we have moved forward in our learning, as in Cesarean section and the R.H. factor in changing the baby's blood. In other ways, however, the constant desire to research reveals something brutal and cruel about today's hospital nurseries. Women changed, with their doctors' help, from the natural instinct to nurse and cuddle their babies to the use of the bottle, allowing them to leave their babies in the care of others. Since some recent studies of crib deaths have revealed bottle milk to be the cause, some mothers are returning to the method nature has intended.

With so many women and babies becoming a part of the medical hospital scene, doctors have been able to build an impressive power structure of cooperation, uniting Mr. and Mrs. Average Citizen to the ever-increasing dictatorship of the medical societies.

In an attempt to unite all of the healing art under one dictatorship monopoly, the knowledge of human psychology has played its part, dolling up the hospitals and doctors' offices with a professional air, building, ever building, the image. With pretentions of maintaining integrity and keeping "quacks" out of the profession, eloquent rhetoric invoked disapproval and contempt of any other method than those of the dictatorship.

During the Second World War, this little article came out, in an attempt to keep the chiropractors from being expelled from the State of Utah, entitled, "The Fifth Freedom:"

> "Do you want to retain your freedom? Of course you do. Who would be so stupid as to choose to give it up? And yet no one can enjoy the privileges of freedom without the responsibility of helping to keep it. Furthermore, one by one, its preci-

ous and protective principles can easily be lost by all of us if we fail to shoulder our part of that responsibility.

"We have heard much of the four freedoms:
1. Freedom of speech.
2. Freedom of press.
3. Freedom from want.
4. Freedom from fear.

None can deny that all of these are equally desirable and essential to our way of life. But indispensable as they are, there is a fifth freedom which is a part of all of them and yet, in importance, seems to over-shadow all the rest. This is the "Freedom of Choice," which gives us the right to choose our occupations, residences, friends, religions, opportunities, stations in life and many other things equally advantageous and desirable. It is this little-talked-of freedom which we must seriously consider and jealously guard, if we are to retain it. Competition in business does much to keep it clean and healthy. The keener the competition, the better service and products we enjoy.

"Monopoly in any field inevitably gives rise to dishonesty in product and service, as well as unfair prices, racketeering and dirty politics. Our government is constantly on the alert to put down monopoly wherever it appears. Should it now be allowed to creep in and take possession over such a priceless factor as our nation's health? Certainly not, you say, but right under our very noses this has already happened in our neighboring state of Idaho and a considerable number of others, where by law, monopoly has taken away the right to practice in the field of health, from all, save one group. And let us be reminded that when there are none left to oppose or question their methods or veracity, regardless of who they are, then relative to health, we are firmly in the grasp of a vicious dictatorship with all its unquestioned evils.

"In all of God's creations, opposing forces complement each other for the good of mankind. Has man now become wiser than his Creator? And where, in such a situation, is our freedom of choice? Are the developments resulting from monoploy any different in one field than another? Will it not bring about the same aforementioned abuses and evils in the field of health?

"With many thousands of our citizens suffering substandard health, and every hospital in the nation filled to overflowing, should any legitimate group of health practitioners seek to shut out the services of all, save their own? The answer is obvious.

"With such preponderous evidence as this existing, unquenched maelstrom of sickness and disease thus tauntingly pointing its lethal finger at all who profess skill in the healing arts, has any one group made progress sufficient to justify the stand that they and they alone should be entrusted to handle a condition so grave and so alarming? Regardless of which group it may be, whether Allopathic (MD), Osteopathic (DP), Chiropcractic (DC), or Naturopathic (ND), can any be allowed dictatorship over America's health? You have only one recourse to prevent such a great tragedy: Whenever it shows its evil head as a political issue, regardless of its disguise, see that your vote insures for you the fifth freedom, the FREEDOM OF CHOICE, because it vitally concerns your most priceless possession, YOUR HEALTH!"

Many have battled and struggled to maintain the truths, while the whole world seemed bent on its absurd course. The gap widened so far between the nature doctor and the medical doctor, as to make it appear that the medical monopoly was in the know, and all else were "quacks."

It is interesting to see how the pendulum has made a complete swing from the time that Oliver Wendell Holmes called all the new chemical doctors "quacks." We are watching now the decline, as the procedures built on such a structure of vanity and professional showmanship fails to get the job done.

We have seen in the past few months the FDA moving quickly to close all vitamin sources of A and D vitamins. Soon it is intended to lower all values in vitamin supplements so that all these so-called "health nuts" will become disenchanted with vitamins; but what appears to be even more sinister, all vitamin therapy is to be brought under the direction of the medical doctor, who knows little or nothing about vitamins, not to mention nutrition. It appears to be a conspiracy between certain factors who fear the loss of prestige, because the people are thinking more and more of natural methods.

The grip of dictatorship is feeling its loss of power with the people. It never ceases to amaze me how certain groups are able to enact laws before they are passed on by Congress. It is even intended to remove, by law, the words "organic" or "natural," so people will not be able to know the difference when they buy, thus attempting to break completely the spirit of the nature doctor and his followers. It almost appears they dictate to the Government.

The FDA is working on the theory that the public is too dumb to know what to eat or what medicines they should take. The FDA regulations in regard to vitamin dosage denies the intelligence of the consumer. They should, in my opinion, place the restrictions on the wholesalesrs to prove their products before they enter the market, knowing toxicity ahead of time, rather than as it has been, for anything and everything to flood the market, food or poison, until eventually the FDA can prove each product to find poison. Every "con" artist and "shister" can do as he pleases until they catch him. And at the rate new chemicals find their way into our foods, that could be never. It looks like the ban on A and D vitamins is only a beginning, starting first with the health food stores and natural products to please the powers that be. Sooner or later, however, if there is any justice left, it will have to hurt the medical doctor as well; the public will demand it.

Then like the young "hippie" the FDA will have to throw down all establishments, good or bad. If there has been a conspiracy, it looks like they will pull the rug right out from under each other. Perhaps it will be a blessing. They will have a hard time keeping us from eating and taking the herbs of the fields for medicine. Then we will have to learn to make a correct choice in food or be sick. We may even learn how to garden organically.

What is the job that really needs to be done? It is not just relief from pain, but rather prevention of pain; not the cutting out until there is nothing left to be cut; not the giving of harmful drugs until the body is wasted and lost. Regardless of their increasing squeeze for power, the next doctor in the spotlight on history's stage will have to be the doctor of preventive medicine, the teacher of truth who will help people to maintain their health.

Yes, the pendulum is on the swing back to nature's own medicine. As Hippocrates said, "Food is your medicine." What a grand and wonderful adventure it will be, as the truth of life begins to come into focus, when people feel well and happy: it will truly usher in the Millenium of real peace on earth. My intention is not to break down all establishments as the young feel to do, but rather to let freedom reign again that other possibilities may be explored, that those old established truths of sound doctrine may be added to, not lost in the shuffle.

With no real statistics available to show the relation of the age of the mothers incident to birth defects, we cannot assume that they are all young people. However, with an age of immorality and perversion which have accompanied the use of drugs, family life has taken a great downward plunge, occuring not only because of the so-called generation gap, but also because of the lack of responsibility that has caused the increase of working mothers.

Like the "Satires of Juvenal" recited in the coliseums of a decaying Rome, making fun of the sickness of homosexuality, so do our comedians the same on stage and TV, in our own sick society. These things contribute to the destruction of the home. But still another sinister sin hangs over our nation like a dark cloud, the sin of abortion. Quoting from the Hippocratic oath, "Neither will I give a woman means to procure an abortion." With the divorce rate and the lack of morals, too many women are left to raise and support the children. The only way many modern women think they can really free themselves from responsibility, as many men have, is to petition for equal rights. This seems to them an easier out than facing the instinctive conscience of a mother looking into the face of a tiny, helpless baby. The *Doctrine and Covenants* tells us, D. & C. 83:

> "Women have claim on their husbands for their mainte- nance, until their husbands are taken;"

It further states,

> "All children have claim upon their parents for their maintenance until they are of age."

What does this all bring us to? What is going to happen if everyone becomes irresponsible? Let me ask another question: What is going to happen when the mineral resources run out and we can no longer get the drugs? There are no second crops of minerals, unfortunately, after the first has been used. The decline of a nation coincides with the using up of natural resources. Then as new rich sources are discovered new wealthy nations rise. Metal output and Rome declined together. During the Dark Ages, mining was almost lost. The Dark Ages ended with the discovery of rich mineral deposits in Central Europe. Venice, as a poverty-stricken fishing village, changed overnight and became a wealthy city because of mining in the north. England's rise to the position of world industrial leader in the 1800's was a result of mining lead (1856), copper (1863), tin (1871), and iron (1882). England supplied the world with more of these metals and mined more coal than any other country in the world.

Then following England, in the 1900's the United States became the top producer of coal, iron, copper, lead, petroleum and other mineral products. Then the resulting chemicals, potash, etc., became the requirements of industry — plastics, glass, chemicals and medicine. We only have one really large source of potash in the U.S., in south-eastern New Mexico. We get some from sea water in California and Utah.

Do you see, we as a nation are in the process of using up the supply which cannot be planted like a crop of potatoes, and the nation is under great stress to supply the ever-increasing demands of a rich, spoiled, self-centered people. It is hard for the rich to realize that there ever is a point when the money runs out. We are like a nation of leeches, like the rich man's son who didn't ever learn the business but spent his dead father's money, lavishly and foolishly, until it ran out, never realizing that he should have used some of it to make an increase. It is my opinion that after the metals run out and the nation declines, we will have new discoveries of metals and chemicals, only when we have profited by the past experience enough to use these treasures to bless mankind, toward a Millenial reign. Brigham Young said in his Discourses on page 305:

> "Wealth belongs to the Lord – Earthly riches are concealed in the elements God has given to man, and the essence of wealth is power to organize from these elements every comfort and convenience of life for our sustenance here, and for Eternal existence hereafter. The possession of all the gold and silver in the world would not satisfy the cravings of the immortal soul of man. The gift of the Holy Spirit of the Lord alone can produce a good, wholesome, contented mind. Instead of looking for gold and silver, look to the heavens and try to learn wisdom until you can organize the native elements for your benefit: then, and not until then, will you begin to possess true riches."

Surely all of these metals and chemicals have been designed for the benefit and wealth of the people of the earth. In our eagerness to use and exploit our fellowmen we have, in many cases, used them to destroy one another, as well as our environment.

The using up of our resources that cannot be planted annually may be the blessing to remove us from the madness of drugs, forcing us to explore those things that can be planted. There have been some very interesting things done with the soy bean for example.

When the attitude changes because a nation falls to her knees and is humbled in the dust, then will a few great men rise as in past times to lift the people and show them a better way. These men seem to be the great thinkers, men of wisdom and learning — the prophets. Men who have an intense desire to help and serve the world; men with the kind of spirit it takes to surmount the problems. Sad but true, after they have lifted and shown the way, there are always the leeches who want to exploit new ideas to make money, leading the nations again to a fall. Let us hope the next time this happens, we will have learned enough by sorrow and sad experience that we will be ready to usher in a millenium where there will be health and peace for all who dwell on the earth.

As petroleum and other of earth's products run out and a nation declines, sometimes it is a long period before a change takes place. Like the Dark Ages, let us hope this time the great men and the finding of new sources or new methods will come forth soon. Truly great thinkers of the past have appreciated and worked with the laws of nature, not against her, as we have done to pollute our world, and destroy one another. With the drug chemicals, we have created another atomic bomb that will destroy us all if we do not make a change; but like my father used to say, "When the outgo exceeds the income, the upkeep becomes the downfall." The outgo of metal, chemicals and petroleum are exceeding the income, and unless new sources are found (and it may be a blessing if they are not), the constant accelerating demand will be the downfall.

Down through history there has been the "charlatan," the "con artist," and the real "quack" ready to make a dollar on the misfortunes of his fellows. But what about today's dictatorship: doctors who call themselves professionals, and have a paper to prove it, but are limited in their assistance to the sick by the powers that be, powers who make money from the chemicals that have become big business. When will the men of real integrity realize that there are other fields to explore, that this one track they are on is killing too many people. The people are beginning to see and are turning more and more to look for something else. As they do, they become easy prey to all the old "con artists" and are gullible to all sorts of cures, groping helplessly from one thing to another as they become disenchanted with drugs.

Let me discuss with you in the next chapter some of the ways I feel you will be able to save yourself in this polluted environment when you are not able to get drugs that you are accustomed to. There will be many who will die if they cannot get certain drugs, "insulin," etc. There will be many who will die if they cannot get the tranquilizers and the pep-ups.

Many will just die as a result of hunger and famine, as their bodies will go through too much of a cleanse, or withdrawal from drugs.

Nature's way of healing is a gradual up-building, but to the impatient it may seem slow. To surrender the indulgences that kill requires sacrifice, but finally nature does her work wisely and well. Those who persevere, obeying her laws, will be rewarded with health of mind and body. There is no way I can convince you, as you will have to convince yourself.

The rewards of obedience will make you a believer. When you come to be a believer, look back deeper than I have shown you into medical history and you will find much pure truth that has been lost in the world of drug superstition we know today. Thomas Edison said,

40

"Until man duplicates a blade of grass, Nature can laugh at his so-called scientific knowledge. Remedies from chemicals will never stand in favourable comparison with the products of Nature – the living cell of the plant, the final result of the rays of the sun, the mother of all life. When correctly used, herbs promote the elimination of waste matter and poisons from the system by simple, natural means. They support Nature in its fight against disease; while chemicals, not being assimilable, add to the accumulation of morbid matter and only simulate improvement by SUPPRESSING the SYMPTOMS."

May the next generation seek to weld the truths of the past and the truth found in today's medical hospitals with the healing powers of faith and nature's medicines, so that the world may be a healthier place in which to live: this is my hopeful reason for writing this book.

As I open to your view some of the things I have learned about nature's wonderful remedies, remember, remedies are only the antidote for law transgressed, a terrestrial law, a remedy to repair the break in the law. Immaculate health comes only by discovery of the law and strict obedience. With a sudden spirit of resolve, we try to obey when we learn nature's secrets. Sometimes we make it for a short while, sometimes a long time and sometimes hardly a moment. If a lasting result could be won, we would have no need of the antidote or even the discovery of said antidote. It is the same with faith to be healed, at times it eludes us on all sides. Health, happiness and a testimony are fleeting things; we have to work at them to keep them.

The more these things are intensely and passionately sought after, with rules obeyed and rewards won, the sooner they become a part of our habit patterns. J. M. Gibby said, "A mistake made more than once is no longer a mistake — it is a habit."

As you learn these things, look at it with hope and courage, not something close to panic when you fail now and then. Faith is only the path to the doorway of the celestial, where perfection dwells. There will be a time when the struggle will all go out of it. Each thing we overcome takes away a part of the struggle, until things will flow to us without compulsory means. D. & C. 121:45, 46:

> "Let virtue garnish thy thoughts unceasingly; then shall thy confidence wax strong in the presence of God; and the doctrine of the Priesthood shall distil upon thy soul as the dews from heaven. The Holy Ghost shall be thy constant companion, and thy scepter an unchanging scepter of righteousness and truth; and thy dominion shall be an everlasting dominion, and without compulsory means it shall flow unto thee forever and ever."

CHAPTER TWO
FASTING — THE GARDEN OF EDEN
TO THE MILLENIUM

As I begin this chapter, I feel much like Johan Miller, 1464, a mathematician and scientist who wrote to a fellow mathematician,

> *"I do not know whither it will run, it will use up all my paper if I do not stop it. One problem after another occurs to me and there are so many beautiful ones, that I hesitate as to which I should submit to you."*

My mind reflects back over the 25 years I have spent in quest for the truths pertaining to the functions of the human body. These things I now present to you with a prayer in my heart that I may bring to your mind some concepts which will be stepping stones to solutions to your health problems and assist you in overcoming the fear that accompanies the lack of knowledge. These things I will teach you have saved my family thousands of dollars in doctor bills and have given us a sense of well being, peace, and security.

So often after a major surgery for cancer, you will hear someone say, "I have been cured." Gibby said,

> *"You may escape immediate punishment for your trans- gression of law but you cannot elude the immutable sting of its gathered power."*

The sad thing we have observed is that the person so cured usually sooner or later dies of cancer. Gibby continues,

> *"Natural death is a gradual process, only its consummation seems sudden."*

To teach you the things about healing which I believe to be true, we must begin with the correct concept of body metabolism and learn just what happens during a fast. Down through history, all truly great men have learned that fasting brings concrete results and tangible gains both physically and spiritually. Plutarch, A.D. 46 to about A.D. 126, said,

"Some men, led by gluttony, rush off to join in drinking bouts, as if they were laying in provisions for a siege. The less expensive foods are always more helpful. When in a precipitate retreat, Artaxerxes Memon had nothing to eat but barley bread and figs, he exclaimed – 'What a pleasure is this, which has never been mine before.' Especially to be feared are indigestions arising from meats, for they are depressing at the outset, and a pernicious residue from them remains behind. It is best to accustom the body not to require meat in addition to other food. The earth yields in abundance many things not only for nourishment but for comfort and enjoyment. But since custom has become a sort of unnatural second nature, our use of meat should be as a prop and support of our diet; we should use other foods – more in accord with nature, and less dulling to the reasoning faculty, which, as it were, kindled from plain and light substance."

43

Galatians 6:7:

"Be not deceived; God is not mocked; for whatsoever a man soweth, that shall he also reap. For he that soweth to his flesh shall of the flesh reap corruption; but he that soweth to the Spirit shall of the Spirit reap life everlasting."

Romans 6:23:

"The wages of sin is death."

Proverbs 13:15:

"The way of the transgressor is hard."

Cicero:

"Youth of sensuality and intemperance delivers over to old age a worn out body."

Brigham Young:

> "When man lives to the age of the tree, his food will be fruit."

Professor Arnold Ehret, in his book Mucusless Diet Healing System, said,

> "Every disease no matter what name it is known by medical science, is constipation, a clogging up of the entire pipe system of the human body. Any special symptom is therefore merely an extraordinary local constipation by more accumulated mucus at this particular place."

What would happen if you found yourself in the office room of a large building where all rooms and hallways were jammed with people? Of course any serious attempt you might make to escape would be futile until some of the people near the exits moved out. We will liken the blood stream to the hallway. When the intake of food is stopped as in fasting, leaving the hallway free, the rooms begin to empty into the outlet, the hallway. If all of the rooms begin to empty at once, the hallway would again become crowded; some in the rooms would still have to wait until the crowd had dispersed. This is a rather crude analogy, but I feel this is exactly what occurs during a fast. The wastes cannot remove themselves because of too much debris in the blood stream (the passageway) and the lymph (the rooms); with too much eating continually, waste remains in the lymph and tissues to rot. Then when an opportunity presents itself for the debris to escape, as in fasting, the person feels awful — as in an acute illness. You have read of people who fasted ten days and then died. They did not die from fasting, but they died of their own filth.

It is like taking a shot of deadly poison. At times the body will become toxic, and subconsciously knowing that it must move the waste or die it somehow forces an elimination to save life — a cold, flu, pneumonia, etc., or acute illness. During the course of an acute illness when waste is on the move in the blood, the person feels all the same effects of a fast, such as weakness, headache, dizziness, etc. — a sort of self-poisoning. If the avenues of elimination, bowel and kidneys, are clogged, the body will turn to other avenues of escape — eyes, ears, nose, throat and skin. If these cannot move it as fast as the body is forcing this exit, a fever will commence and move it out in the form of heat, possibly like running a car fast with its brakes on. This has been called a disease crisis. This type of crisis nature forces upon us in order to save our lives, and even bacteria is a means to help expedite the elimination of waste. Fasting can bring about the same thing. When too much waste is moved, too rapidly, the result can be death, as an acute illness can also cause death. This is why a gradual change in diet with short periodic fasting is a better way to clear and clean the body, along with herbs and mild food.

If you can begin to see the vision of how the body heals itself and can begin to learn the true and correct body metabolism, you will understand that when the body is clean and free from waste and is properly nourished, you have no need to fear the microbe. Bacteria does not live on sound, healthy tissue. Professor Ehret said,

> "Metabolism, or the 'science of change of matter,' is the most absurd and the most dangerous doctrine-teaching ever imposed on mankind."

When an attempt is made to disprove or even challenge traditional belief deeply rooted in the consciousness of a society, profound anguish seems to be a part of the conflict. Even if truth is brought to the foreground, there are always those who would prevent the departure of age-old fables and half truths, because it is too difficult a thing to change established habits so as to conform to a new-found truth. The rejection of truth is often only a weakness of the individual who dares not find out if it is true because it may virtually change the old habit pattern. Too often we live in such a rut as to not have any desire to change no matter how it could change our lives for the good. There are those who would have their drink or their junk food if it kills them, and it usually does.

Let me propose a replacement for some of these age-old ideas with some sound truths, some of which will seem strangely difficult. But if learned and used, they can and will carry you on to beautiful, immaculate health. You may be annoyed in this next paragraph to discover that I do not believe the protein theory as such. Before you put this book down and refuse to learn my reasons for this statement, let us view some of the testimonies of people who have walked in this direction.

There have been a few health resorts set in the United States, many in Europe and other countries, that have had amazing results from a natural diet program. Many people who had been given up to die have found new life by a return to natural raw fruits, vegetables, and herbs. The intensely interesting fact which strongly links all such places is the lack of high protein foods with a total result of many miracle recoveries. Often these people who have been restored to health find, for the first time in their lives, an exhilarating sense of well being they have not known in their entire lifetime, so they continue on in this sustained way of life, without the heavy proteins. The other fact which links these natural methods of healing is the use of raw or mostly raw food. These people who have learned some of the main secrets of the healing art know that live raw foods are nature's best healers.

While working in one of these natural healing sanitariums many years ago, I watched miracles performed. One woman who had tumors of the uterus began using raw food, three days of vegetables and fruit and four days of grapes and grapejuice per week, for six weeks. One day while taking a sitz bath, she said, "Something is happening to me." Suddenly, the mass of tumor came out into the water and I put it into a specimen bottle and took it to the doctor. This same woman's mother was healed of cancer in six weeks on a grape diet. As I watched these things, I became deeply fascinated by what I saw, and I started a study which has proven to me beyond a shadow of a doubt that fasting and a fruit diet, or a fruit and vegetable diet, preferably raw, is the only way the body will heal.

I have told many people about the things I've learned, and many have had the courage to try it — usually not, however, until they have exhausted all medical possibilities. As soon as they began to obey these simple rules, the body began to heal, even in cases where the doctors had given them up to die, or where they had spent thousands of dollars on doctor bills. One woman I talked to had done just that, spent much money and time going from one doctor to another on account of a skin disease her daughter had had a long time. After stopping the intake of protein, starch, and sugar and going to fruits and vegetables, the girl's skin cleared to the amazement of the mother. Another woman in her seventies was just released from the hospital, having had bleeding ulcers. Her appearance was sickly and pale and weak; having received no real help from the doctors, she decided to give natural methods a try. Using a quart of raw cabbage juice a day, high Vitamin C and okra tablets before each meal of fruits and vegetables, she looked well again in no time at all. When she went back to the doctor for a check up, he could not believe the progress she had made in two weeks, so he asked her what she had been doing. When she told him, he said, "Well, whatever you are doing, better keep it up." This woman and I had lunch together not too long ago, and she was eating a raw green salad. I asked her if she ever had any more stomach ulcers since that time, almost nine years ago, and she said she could eat anything. Usually after seeing the results of raw food, people tend to try harder to live with more of them than they have in the past.

A man I knew was a bishop, a school principal, and had a side business which kept him very busy; he developed a bad case of arthritis of the knee and spine. I told him about carrot and celery juice as an aid, so he tried the canned carrot juice with no help. When I reminded him again, he was completely flat on his back and told me the canned juice did not work, so I offered to loan him my juicer. I took it to their house and showed his wife how to use it. She gave him a quart of carrot juice and a quart of celery juice, raw, for two weeks and kept him off starches and sweets; by the end of two weeks, the pain was gone. Because he was so elated with this new-found truth, he went right out and bought his family a juicer. The third week was fast meeting in church, and he got up and thanked me publicly in his testimony and told everyone they ought to have a juicer.

One time a man I had met, who was in his sixties, all bent with arthritis of the spine and arms, suffered excruciating pain. After living a few weeks with raw juices and a fruit and vegetable diet, relief from pain was his reward. He said to me one day, "How soon can I go back to eating like I did before?" I told him what he did was up to him. When he returned to his old ways of eating, the pain returned and he didn't feel well again, so he decided to go back on the fruit and vegetable diet. In as short a time as three months, he had no more arthritis pain and also had the reward of passing great black pieces of chronic waste from his lungs.

A woman I met who went on a fruit, vegetable, and herb diet passed a large tumor from the bowel within about three months. Later she passed tumors from the vaginal area and also from the lungs. The last time I saw her, she looked wonderful; and from her conversation I knew she was totally converted to the idea of a fruit and vegetable diet.

There was a little girl I knew who, at two months of age, began to have seizures. After extensive tests with the EEG, showing that the brain was under constant seizure, she was released from the hospital. The doctors did not know what was wrong or what to do. One neurologist even said she would be better off dead. The parents were given phenobarbitol and dilantin and sent home with their baby with no hope. The parents, having nowhere else to go, decided to try natural methods and learned from the child's eyes that she had an inner ear infection draining into the brain. They gave the child a cleansing diet of raw goat milk and honey, high doses of vitamin C, fruit, herb teas, and enemas. The child began to drain mucus and after two weeks there were no more seizures. These people have been doubly blessed in being able to keep their little girl but have also learned some hidden treasures which

47

will bless them and all of their children. Their testimony will also be a blessing to others seeking answers.

Another woman I knew had had a severe kidney infection for some time and, being in her seventies, I suppose she just thought sickness was part of the trial that went with age. After learning about the mild food diet and the kidney herbs, she began to test their theories. She had the courage few people ever achieve and stayed on it for a year. When I went to visit after many months, I noticed she had new carpet and new paint on the walls. After telling her how wonderful she looked, she said, "I feel just wonderful and I've even painted my house." She had found some hidden treasures that few have the discernment or the courage to find.

I have seen and read about many cases of skin conditions, chronic hay fever, asthma, arthritis, cancer, tumors, leukemia and most of the so-called incurable terminal diseases cleansed from peoples' bodies. As obstacles were patiently overcome, a whole new physical rehabilitation took place. When they continue to live on vital, raw, live foods, an effervescence and an aura of vigorous buoyancy, like the healthy young, sends out sparks of energy in all directions. People who have tried it and have remained on these foods also develop an energy of spirit that is beautiful to behold.

48

You may say to me, "What about protein? We need to have protein." A woman came to see me one time and told me this story: Her 18-year-old son on graduation night was in an accident where he was thrown from his car; she said, "He was like jello thrown on the ground." His body was so split open in front that he was only able to be fed intravenously. After some time with no improvement, tests were made showing that the protein in his body was too low for him to live. Any attempt to feed him meat was impossible. His mother, knowing about raw juice therapy, asked the doctor if she could give him carrot juice. The doctor agreed she could try anything, as he felt that he had done all he could. Having spent most of the summer at the hospital with her boy, his health only becoming worse and worse, it was a rewarding experience after a few weeks on raw vegetable juices for her to be able to take him home. Upon leaving the hospital the doctor said, "Don't expect him to walk for at least three years." After three weeks of nothing but raw juices, the woman and her son arrived at the hospital for a check up. To the amazement of the staff, the boy was walking again. After another protein check they found it to be perfect. Where did the protein come from?

You may say, "What about amino acids? If we do not need the protein as we have been taught, surely we need the amino acid in meat."

Our bodies are made up of protein and amino acids. Have you ever noticed that in the beautiful order in nature, God places necessary things in each animal, plant, or human being so as not to inflict casualty. We are all so fragile and breakable, and yet we live, move, and have our being without the concern of melting away like butter when we go out in the sun. No, I personally, after observing many people in a fasting condition and after fasting extensively many times myself, up to as many as 21 days (and there are many who have fasted 40-50 days), cannot accept what the protein believers would have me believe: that as soon as you fast, your body begins to eat up its own protein. The interesting thing about fasting is this: the greatest fasters, those who have fasted the longest and easiest, are the thin type. Where is the "eating up" in this case? Starvation is a different thing entirely, where no new foods, vegetable or animal, are introduced into the body for an extended period until the body does not have any more fuel. The protein of which the body is made begins to deteriorate, with death as the result. If fuel is added before deterioration goes too far, the body will begin the process of becoming a protein healthy flesh again out of the fuel used, not protein to make protein, but fuel to maintain life. This is the life process. All heavy protein foods must make a change in the body before they can be used; this is a well-known fact. Could it be that a change could also convert vegetables and fruits into protein flesh? A cow eats grass all day and makes protein flesh. A bird eats worms and makes protein flesh. A guinea pig eats mostly lettuce and vegetables and makes protein flesh. Cats and carnivorous animals eat meat and make protein flesh; but it may just be possible that humans can do both. The reason we have so many incurable diseases is that medical science has not figured this out yet. A person who has Cushing's Disease, for instance, cannot in the later stages handle meat at all, because they lack the hormone allowing them to make the change accurately. I will show you later why this is so.

49

No, the theories of man do not agree with sound logic. Could it be that the reason for amino acids in meat, etc., is because, like our bodies, they are made up of amino acids and protein? Or could it be in the order of things that when we eat the flesh foods or any food with amino acids, it is a necessary part to aid us in the use of such foods in our bodies?

I have personally found, and many others have also, that while living on a fruit and vegetable diet the body does not require amino acids and will easily and readily convert body tissue into the proteins and amino acids of which it is made up. I have nursed babies while living strictly on a fruit and nut diet and made wonderful protein milk and had beautiful protein babies. You may say, "You made the milk from the nuts you ate." Do not misunderstand me — I am not saying we do not need any protein foods. Nuts, however, are a fruit and do not have the amino acids of meat. That there is a certain amount of protein in fruits and vegetables, and here again in the correct order and amounts, tells me that certainly by the law of nature we need this amount of protein; but because our bodies are made up of protein does not mean it requires a lot of protein to build the body. Then again the fuel may not be building protein at all. There may be another answer. However, there is a difference in the kind of fuel we use — too much concentrated food and too much eating cause sludge, like the result of burning poor gasoline in your car.

Everything in nature changes from one thing to make another; it does not make the same thing out of the same thing. The high protein theory, when used in chronic or acute disease, clogging the system as it attempts to heal, is as Professor Ehret said, ". . . borders on insanity."

There are many wonderful things that occur during a fast. You may be interested to know that one of the first things that happens after a few days of fasting is, you will feel pain wherever chronic disease is lodged in the body, thereby pinpointing the area, while all other body discomfort — aches and pains, swelling, etc., will disappear. When a person has no chronic disease, all aches and pains from normal eating will vanish; the body feels good and free from pain of any kind.

You can watch the tongue become coated whiter and whiter as the body moves waste into the blood. The tongue will become as white as during an acute illness. Professor Ehret calls the tongue the "magic mirror." The magic mirror shows how badly encumbered the body is with waste. When the fast is broken, the tongue will clear as elimination is brought to a halt. There are many kinds of fasts which will bring a good result — water, fruit juice, fruit, lemon honey, and water and herb teas. In the use of water and herb teas only during a fast, disease moves more slowly and is easier on all vital organs. Short fasts in conjunction with mild food, herbs, and vitamins, giving the body a chance to cleanse and build more slowly at the same time, is the best way. Sometimes during a fast the body forces more toxic matter than usual and causes an acute condition; a change to fruit, enemas, and vitamin C is then helpful. Using fruit must be done with caution, as fruit loosens and moves mucus waste very rapidly in cases where there is chronic disease. It may move so fast as to cause much trouble, even death. During the process we call acute disease though, fruit or fruit juice is best as fruit not only loosens but dissolves mucus, allowing it to pass more easily through the kidneys. Nature in this case has already forced an elimination, one which could be too much for the body to live through; so it is wise then to help her all we can to get the waste out the quickest and best way — herbs, laxatives, enemas, vitamin C, fruit and fruit juice only.

When a forced elimination occurs (acute disease), the body temporarily changes from a feeding organ to an eliminative organ. Any feeding will only hinder nature in her determined course, that of emptying the waste to save your life. Care should be taken in breaking a long fast, using first a laxative, an enema and then a vegetable meal, mostly raw. I do not believe in long fasts however, I am always in favor of doing things the easiest, most comfortable way — with herbs and mild food. The best authority I know of teaching the correct principle of fasting is Professor Ehret. Two of his books are, *Mucusless Diet Healing System* and *Physical, Mental and Spiritual Rejuvenation*. Professor Ehret, after healing his own body of Bright's Disease and consumption through fasting when he was given up to die as a young man, learned these principles through his own experience and through the experiences of the many thousands of people he helped. I have proven over and over in the past 25 years that what he taught about how the body feeds and eliminates is exactly correct. Whether I have found all the reasons why it is correct, I do not know. I only know it is true. There are those who see the value of fasting, cleansing the body with fruits and vegetables and go about it with suspicious enthusiasm, but who can not seem to give their full attention to as difficult a problem as changing habit patterns and acquired tastes. Then there are those I have seen who start out with a bang, see the value and tell everyone they know who will listen, but fall too quickly back into the old habits of permissive indulgence. Those who stick it out and stay with it find the most marvelous rewards for obedience to nature's own laws. The development of strength has many of its own reqards — courage, spirituality, character, individuality — not to mention fantastic health. Those who see the truth but are nudged and prodded by social opinion wind up like a phrase attributed to Confucius: "He that goes the middle of the road gets hit on both sides." They are to be pitied. Social relations become increasingly tense until they go one way or the other. Usually people of this type, after being steadily undermined, gradually fall back into old habits more acceptable to the environment around them.

Let me at this point quote Brigham Young from the Journal of Discourses 13:142:

"*As we get richer and build warm houses, and have lived*

more richly, indulging in *sweet cake, plum pudding, roast beef and so on, we have had more or less disease among us.*"

Journal of Discourses 12:37:

"*Go into their houses and you will find beef, pork, apple pie, custard pie, pumpkin pie, mince pie, and every luxury, and they live so as to shorten their days and the days of their children. You may think that these things are not of much importance; no more they are, unless they are observed, but let the people observe them and they lay the foundation for longevity, and they will begin to live out their days, not only a hundred years, but by and by, hundreds of years on the earth. Do you think they will stuff themselves then with tea and coffee, and perhaps with a little brandy sling before breakfast and a little before going to bed, and then beef, pork, mutton, sweet meats, and pastry, morning and noon and night? No; you will find they will live as our first parents did, on fruits and on a little simple food, and they will never overload the stomach.*

And as has been mentioned before, Journal of Discourses 8:63:

"*When men live to the age of a tree, their food will be fruit.*"

It is my hope to be able to show you that it is possible for man to live on fruit and vegetables, or fruit only, to maintain beautiful, immaculate health. I hope also to be able to show you why and how man could live to the age of the tree under these circumstances.

Because we seem to have such a variety of foods to eat and because, for the most part, we have the opportunity during our lifetime to partake of this variety, we make a garbage pail of our stomachs without regard to whether all elements in food of such variety will combine. When the scientist works among chemicals he is always careful of combinations lest he find himself in outer space. Something about our inner knowledge that we have always existed makes us feel that we can eat anything or do anything to our body, and it will last and last. Not even the sight of a friend or neighbor layed away has any lasting effect on us; we seem to suffer from the illusion that our friend's misfortune cannot possibly happen to us. Not until after we have abused our body for some time does nature finally ring the alarm. But what do we do? We take an aspirin or some other pain killer and say, "No, I will not hear of this," or, "I would rather die than not be able to have that." We bring upon ourselves all the misery of disease because we refuse to find out what manner of fuel is required by our body, much less how to use it in the correct combinations and amounts.

To discover what man ate in the beginning, may we go back to the time of Adam and Eve in the Garden. Genesis 1:29:

> "And God said, Behold, I have given you every herb bearing seed, which is upon the face of the earth, and every tree, in the which is the fruit of the tree yielding seed; to you it shall be for meat."

We see that man was intended to live on fruits and herbs. This was the law of Eden. Then as we watch man evolving into a wicked creature, his diet and habits change until he becomes so wicked the Lord decided to remove him from the earth, with the exception of a few.

After Noah and his family leave the Ark and erect an altar of prayer before the Lord, the word of the Lord again gives a command about man's diet — this time, however, not so strict a diet. He tells man,

Genesis 9:3-4:

> "Every moving thing that liveth shall be meat for you; even as the green herb have I given you all things. But flesh with the life thereof, which is the blood thereof, shall ye not eat. And surely your blood of your lives will I require; at the hand of every beast will I require it, and at the hand of man; at the hand of every man's brother will I require the life of man."

Genesis 6:3:

> "And the Lord said, My spirit shall not always strive with man, for that he also is flesh; yet his days shall be an hundred and twenty years."

We can see now with this diet his life span is shortened. Now man is free to eat all things. Perhaps he had reached such a stage that he could no longer live the highest law so was given the free reign to do with his body as he chose and eat whatever pleased him which, of course, he did. There then came a time when God desired a purer, finer race of people to whom he could give the Priesthood, to whom he could give special light and truth, upon whom he could bestow special favor, a chosen people (Israel), a people who would bless the entire earth. To this people, through Moses, he gave a special dietary law — Leviticus 11:1-47 and Deuteronomy 14:1-29.

Many of the things required in this law of Moses have been proven worthy of recognition today by science, but many choose to disregard even the findings of science and continue to eat swine's flesh and many of the other things such as shrimp and shell fish, etc., and many lose their lives for this disregard. Brigham Young said,

Journal of Discourses 12:192:

"If the people were willing to receive the true knowledge from heaven in regard to their diet, they would cease to eating swine's flesh. I know this as well as Moses knew it, and without putting it in a code of commandments."

The Lord also gave laws of sanitation through Moses to Israel to make her a cleaner, purer, more righteous people. The Judicial laws that were given have been unsurpassed in all succeeding generations of time; and if we were only using a portion of this law, we would have a superior government. However, man chooses not to live by the commands of God and goes his own way to his own destruction. This is the freedom God has given us, but sooner or later we must bow to the inevitable and obey the law or be destroyed by it.

54

It seems sad when we cannot learn from past mistakes to obey the laws upon which each blessing is predicated. Again through the Prophet Joseph Smith, man is given the Word of Wisdom, D. & C. 89. A more difficult law than the law of Moses, it brings mankind closer to the law of the Garden of Eden and full circle back to the millenial law.

Brigham Young said,

Journal if Discourses 8:63:

"If the days of man are to begin to return, we must cease all extravagant living. When men live to the age of a tree, their food will be fruit. Mothers to produce offspring full of life and days, must cease drinking liquor, tea, and coffee, that their systems may be free from bad effects. If every woman in this Church will now cease drinking tea, coffee, liquor, and all other powerful stimulants, and live upon vegetables, etc. not many generations will pass away before the days of man will again return. But it will take generations to eradicate entirely the influences of deleterious substances."

He mentions other times that the people should eat their bread stale or hard crust. Those who have been wise in all generations of time have known better than to eat hot bread, pancakes, hot pies, biscuits, etc. Brigham Young said,

> "Mothers, keep the children from eating meat; and let them eat vegetables that are fully matured, not unripe, and bread that is well-baked, not soft."

This brings us to the subject of food combinations and why some combinations bring about resulting sickness. The blessing of health and strength is the most coveted of all, to be able to move about without pain or restriction — when health is lost, all seems lost. Let us not be contemptuous of law and order. All things exist in order. There are laws pertaining to combinations of food also.

Have you ever watched a cow or horse eat from morning until evening and wondered how he gets away with that much eating. We could do the same if our diet was as it was in the Garden of Eden: fruit and herbs. This type of food is quickly digested, assimilated, and eliminated from the body; this would naturally require more eating during a day, at least at first, until the body is cleansed. Fruit and fruit juice can be digested and in the blood stream in from 20 to 30 minutes. On the other hand, starch and meat takes from four to six hours to digest and make sufficient change to enter the blood. Pork takes nine hours to digest.

The thing we have not learned from the sad experience of a sour, upset stomach after eating a bowl of chile, or cereal with fruit, is that keeping a fruit, which by nature was intended to leave the stomach within a half hour, in the digestive system until the starch or meat is digested causes all the food in the stomach to putrify and rot. By the time it reaches the small intestines where the absorption takes place, we have going into the blood a putrified, rotted source of nourishment; and we wonder why we do not feel well. It is a well-established fact that people live a good part of their lives after 35 with an upset, sour stomach. This is why so many antacids are sold each year to neutralize the effects of wrong combinations. There are two reasons for the acid: (1) the wrong combinations, and (2) as we approach middle age, having abused our bodies and overworked the sorting processes, causing a tremendous stress, the glands lose much of their strength and vitality to perform.

However, we like the taste of cherry pie, apple pie, and other fruit pies; orange juice with our cereal; toast with fruit; beans with tomato sauce; and a sandwich with tomato on it; and we continue to pay the price of our folly. If on an average diet, we could even learn to eat our foods in the correct combinations, we would help to maintain health. If we could learn to eat 90 per cent mild food and 10 per cent concentrated, and in the correct combinations, there would be much less sickness.

The following chart is to show how to combine foods correctly, on the average diet. This is not a diet I advocate — it only shows most all foods that are eaten and places them in correct combination.

Combine A & B, or A & C   NEVER Combine B & C

A

VEGETABLES		FATS & OILS (not over 3 a meal)
Root	**Greens**	
Beets	Asparagus	Avocados
Celery Root	Artichokes (Cone)	Butter
Carrots	Beans (String)	Cream
Kohlarabi	Beet tops	Coconut (Dried)
Parsnips	Brocolli	Egg Yolks
Radishes	Brussel Sprouts	Fats (Animal)
Rutabagas	Cabbage	Ice Cream
Salsify (Oyster Plant)	Cauliflower	Lard
Turnips	Celery	Nuts (Ex. Chestnuts)
	Chard	Oil (Cod Liver)
Salad	Eggplant	Oil (Olive)
Cabbage	Kale	Oil (Vegetable)
Celery	Kraut	
Watercress	Lettuce	**Sugar**
Cucumber	Mushrooms	(one or two a meal)
Endive	Okra	
Garlic	Peas (Green)	Bananas (Ripe)
Kraut	Peppers (Green)	Brown Sugar
Lettuce	Pumpkin	Dates
Melons	Spinach	Figs
Onions	Squash	Honey
Parsley	Baking Squash	Ice Cream (raw milk, honey)
Spinach	Potato (Baked)	Maple Syrup or sugar
	Yams (Baked)	Prunes
	Sweet Potato (Baked)	Raisins

B

STARCHES
(ONLY ONE A MEAL)

Artichokes	Gravies (Flour)	
Bread (Whole Grain)	Macaroni	
Bread (White)	Oatmeal	
Cereals (Whole Grain)	Pastries	
Cereals (Refined)	Parsnips (Boiled)	
Chestnuts (Cooked)	Peanuts	
Corn (Matured)	Rice (Whole)	
Cornstarch	Spaghetti	
Flour (Whole Grain)	Soups (Thick)	
Flour (White)	Potato (Boiled)	

SWEETS

Candies
Ice Cream
Jellies
Jams
Preserves
Syrups (Refined)
White Sugar

C

PROTEINS
(only one a meal)

Beans (Dried)
Brains
Butter Beans (Green)
Buttermilk
Cheese (Dairy)
Cheese (Cottage)
Clams
Crabs
Egg (Whole)
Fish
Game
Kidneys
Lentils (Sprouted)
Lima Beans (Green)

Liver
Meats
Milk
Nuts (Ex. Chestnuts)
Oysters
Peas (Dried, Sprouted)
Soya Beans (Sprouted)

FRUITS

Apples
Apricots
Berries
Cherries

Currants
Grapes
Grapefruit
Kumquats
Lemons
Limes
Mangoes
Oranges
Peaches
Persimmons
Pineapple
Plums
Pomegranates
Tangerines
Tomatoes

57

Joseph Smith said,

D.H.C. 4:414:

"*I preached to a large congregation at the stand, on the science and practice of medicine, desiring to persuade the Saints to trust in God when sick, and not in an arm of flesh, and live by faith and not by medicine, or poison; and when they were sick, and had called for the Elders to pray for them, and they were not healed, to use herbs and mild food."*

Let us define mild food and see why this is the basis of all healing. We have already discussed how rapidly fruits are digested and removed from the body, from 20 to 30 minutes. Vegetables (not having heavy starch) will digest within 45 to 60 minutes. When used alone, a certain amount of starch is the cause for it taking longer than fruit to digest and be eliminated from the body. Vegetables, however, are moved faster and digested much more easily than the more concentrated foods such as starch, meat, and sugars. These concentrated foods cause the body to work much harder and for a longer period of time, from four to six hours in the process of digestion.

This should bring us to the logical conclusion that whenever any of the bodily functions are impaired in any way, mild foods are more easily digested and moved out of the body, taking debris with them in the process (since both fruit and vegetables, especially those high in ascorbic acid, dissolve mucus). This is much like the action of a detergent on an engine to clean it: The debris and mucus has chronically lodged itself; then the natural oils of the vegetables and fruits found in the skins and seeds and roughage acts like the additive molybdenum disulfide used in engines to reduce the friction and cause longer life of the engine. So it is in the human engine. It has been popular to use a soft poly-unsaturated oil to move cholesterol from the blood for this reason. Cholesterol is nothing more than mucus waste. The natural oils provide a finer lubricating fluid for all internal organs which do not become hardened or lodge themselves as to the harder oils found in meat, eggs, and hydrogenated or cooked oils. Fruit and nut oils can even become hardened and more easily lodged along artery walls when cooked. Nuts or oil-producing fruit and vegetables, skins of apples, etc., harden when cooked, so are better eaten raw.

So for less friction and a more natural lubrication of the body organs, raw fruits, vegetables, nuts, and soft raw oils should be used. Less labor to digest and change is required in order for them to be utilized, especially in a sick body already fatigued by debris and toxic waste accumulated over years of too many concentrated, constipating foods.

It is also logical to use mild food in case of chronic or acute illness, as it requires an adequate amount of hormones, hydrochloric acid, enzymes, etc., to bring the concentrated foods into the state where they can be used by the body during this four-to-six-hour process of digestion. Most people who are chronically sick do not have an adequate hormone balance so as to accurately make this change. With the inability to make this change accurately there is an increase in the toxic waste. Fruit and honey are already glucose sugar and do not need much change. Vegetables have a small amount of starch but still do not require as much body effort in the process of digestion; they also have a cleansing and lubricating action, making them a suitable food for building as well as cleansing, with a minimum strain on body organs.

There are five main types of foods to be removed from the diet of the sick in order for healing to take place. We will call them concentrated or mucus-forming foods. As long as any of these foods are being taken into the body, *chronic waste* will not be eliminated unless it reaches such a state of waste as to destroy the life; then at this stage, nature will force an elimination, as with a cold, flu, or any acute disease. Nature will still, during this forced elimination, not dig too deeply into chronic disease; she will only take off enough waste to allow life to go on. In order to clean the body to immaculate and beautiful health, mild food, herbs, or fasting are the only way. As soon as you start on mild food and herbs, you will prove this to yourself. The body will start to eliminate mucus and waste from all avenues of escape. Your nose will drain if chronic disease is in the head area. As your body begins to clear, you will begin to have good and bad days. If your vitality (or your ability to eliminate) is high, you will immediately feel as though you were acutely ill. These bad days only last a short time, as nature only takes off the top. Then you will feel wonderful, often the way you felt at your best in youth. The world will look new, young, and bright as hope for renewal of health begins to come into focus.

Then the bad days again, as nature digs deeper into the body to root out the chronic disease. Then again, the good days as nature gives you rest in between. As the bad days become further and further apart you know you are on the mend. If vitality is low you will feel better at first until the elimination starts, sometimes taking as long as three weeks. Soon you will hardly be able to remember how bad you had felt in the past, and when you do have a bad day it will be a great annoyance to you.

An acute illness is any illness that puts you in bed: weakness, dizziness, headache, cold, fever, or any virus disease. In defining acute illness, let me give you a completely new concept. A cold, etc., is nature's way of saving your life. We will call it a nature-forced elimination. When you begin to understand this, you will learn to overcome the fear of disease. You will realize that nature is merely trying to save your life. So the next time you have a cold, enjoy it and remember you had it coming, you earned it. Let nature do her work, such a marvelous work; and you can help her as you learn the rules.

Because medical science has found all the bacteria and know not what it feeds upon, it is explained away as being a necessary outcome of conditions of life on this planet, the one form of life must live on another so as to keep a balance of all life on earth, an epidemic being a disaster to man but a triumphant victory for the virus. They talk of resistance to disease but do not really understand what resistance is. To build an immunity by inoculation has been the lesser of two evils but is not the answer. To rid the body of the cause, the food for bacteria, we immediately achieve a true resistance to disease.

God did not place us here to be battered about by all manner of germs, to take our chances. When we learn the rules upon which our bodies were created and learn to live by them, real health will make its appearance on the stage of history.

Chronic disease is as the dictionary defines it: lasting a long time, also recurring, habits that resist all efforts to eradicate them, fixedness, deep-seated, aversion to change and is not easily uprooted nor changed. It is waste lodged in different areas of the body. The only way chronic disease waste will eliminate is by stopping the intake of highly concentrated foods, or fasting, emptying the hallways. The reason why medical science is not able to relieve the intense suffering of chronic disease is because they do not understand what it is, much less how to loosen it from its permanent residence.

As your body begins to eliminate the waste and clear and clean itself on a mild food diet, you can begin to fast periodically on short 24-hour fasts. In the beginning you should eat more vegetables than fruits; as you feel better and better, you can begin to eat more fruit, as fruit draws and loosens the waste too rapidly.

All my life I had been told that fruit cleanses and vegetables build. I do not anymore believe this. Fruit is the builder, cleanser, healer and most perfect food for man. Vegetables slow down the process of elimination somewhat, and concentrated foods bring it to a screeching halt. While your body is cleansing, if you eat the concentrated foods, you will halt the process of elimination. Do not misunderstand me. I am not advocating that you live always on fruit. This is an individual thing. I am merely directing your thinking toward a new and different concept.

Personally, I have found fruit to be the perfect food. A fruit diet, or a long fast, however, can destroy in the case of extreme illness because too much waste moves into the blood, as I have explained. Herbs and mild food may be used without concern, however, where the body is chronically sick. The body will heal, using only mild food. I have seen this happen time and time again. The body will heal using various herbs, and an average diet. I have also seen this, but the combination of herbs and mild food is unbeatable.

Listed now will be the foods I regard as mild foods:

MILD Food in Chronic Sickness   NO Concentrated Foods When Sick

All fruits and vegetables	Grain
(as much raw as possible)	Sugar
Fruit juice (canned, raw, or frozen)	Dairy products
Vegetable juice (raw only)	Butter
Soft oil (raw, cold pressed)	Eggs
All nuts (must be raw)	Dried legumes
Honey (raw)	Meat
Sprouts (alfalfa, bean, grains)	Peanuts
All starch vegetables must be baked	—Chips, etc.
potato, squash, parsnips, yams	

When grain and beans, etc., are sprouted, nature changes them from a starch to a glucose sugar vegetable. As has been explained, the chronically ill do not have the powers of correct hormone balance to change the heavy starch in their own bodies. If nature can make the change ahead of time, before they enter the body, they become a perfect fuel.

When milk products are placed in the sick adult body, they only add mucus. The protein requirements for man are definitely proven by the changes occuring in the milk of the mother at different stages in the development of the child. The amount of protein in the milk diminishes as the child grows older. Starting at 2.38 per cent protein at birth, it diminishes to 1.07 per cent protein by six months of age.

Cow's milk is 16 per cent protein. This could explain the crib deaths from bottle-fed babies; suffocation caused from too much milk and too much high protein. Babies have an enzyme, gastric lipase, which digests fat in the stomach. This lasts about three years.

In an adult the liver bile digests the fat; with the heavy mucus building from high protein diets, most adults only compound the problem the liver already has to cope with by adding milk to their diets. When there are problems with the powers of digestion, as in hormone balance, tumors, or cancer, milk only becomes an added burden. Let me explain how milk can be used, or the dried grains (mush, bread, etc.) in a fasting cleanse, say during a famine. If it is used only as:

1 glass of milk a day, or
1 bowl of mush a day, or
1 slice of bread a day

along with sprouted grain to give the necessary vitamin C, the body will start its process of elimination, because it is now living in a semi-fasting state. During a famine condition, many people will begin this process of elimination and become ill. Thinking they are dying of starvation, rather than relaxing to let nature do her work, they will become fearful; and fear does strange things. During the great plagues of the past, I feel sure that fear killed more people than the plague did.

You may choose the mild food as a cleansing diet, or you may want to use the above concentrated foods in the given amounts.

The following will tell you what happens during a healing crisis versus a disease crisis. As you begin to clean your body, you may, after about three months, experience a healing crisis. You will learn that a healing crisis is brought on by obedience to the rules of cleansing the body and that a disease crisis comes as a result of disobedience to the laws of good health. The only ways the body will heal is through the following: (1) fasting, (2) semi-fasting, (3) forced elimination. There is no other way.

HEALING CRISIS

1. Happens only as the body is naturally cleansed through fasting and/or semi-fasting and correct body-building foods.

2. Happens only when the body has enough vitality to stand the shock.

3. Happens when a person feels the best.

4. Usually takes about three months of correct eating to bring about a healing crisis.

5. Only lasts two or three days at most. No need to take enema or help in

any way, except to stop eating.

6. Sometimes, by correct eating, semi-fasting, etc., the body picks off the waste a little at a time, and no crisis is necessary.

DISEASE CRISIS

1. Happens when the body is too full of mucus and clogged to the limit.

2. Happens when enough germs are multiplying.

3. Happens when body strength and vitality are lowest.

4. Happens to save the life. If clogging continues at the rate it is going, the person would die because of injury to body organs. Poisons in the blood and pumping through the heart, crowding vital organs as in cancer, etc.

5. Lasts several weeks.

6. Happens, sometimes when the body becomes extremely cold, causing the body to squeeze like a sponge, starting an elimination.

FRUITS

1. Loosen waste
2. Sustain the body
3. Cleanse

VEGETABLES

1. Slow down process of
   elimination somewhat
2. Sustain the body
3. Cleanse

PROTEIN TESTS
(When living on mild food)

A. When low
   1. Not enough live food
   2. Not enough herbs to move waste
   3. Obstructions

B. When normal
1. Waste is moving out normally
2. Sufficient raw food and herbs
are being taken

CONCENTRATED FOODS

1. **Do not** loosen waste as do fruits
2. Sustain the body
3. Cleanse (only in semi-fasting proportions)
1 glass milk daily or
1 sandwich daily or
1 bowl of wheat daily, etc.

4. Stop process of elimination somewhat

5. Sustain when taken in normal amounts and with correct food combinations.

6. When taken in excessive amounts,
   a. clog the system
   b. create mucus and pus
   c. chronic disease
   d. create food for parasites and germs.
   (When parasites and germs have enough mucus, etc., to feed on, they multiply. When they have grown enough, nature forces an elimination to save our lives.)

I hope by this time you are beginning to catch the vision of this wonderful hidden treasure. When the light and truth of it begin to dawn on your consciousness, the fear of sickness will begin to fade from you. It will all seem so simple, you will wonder why you did not see it before. When you see someone **feeding** a sick person concentrated food, you will be as shocked as I am; and for a moment, you will wonder why they do not know any better.

Because we have been taught so well and so long that protein is the builder, the minute there is a meat shortage, people panic. If they begin to eat more vegetables and fruits and less and less of the more concentrated foods, they would begin to eliminate poisons and become ill — then they would really believe they were being killed. It becomes very clear to me why, as the Prophets have foretold, there will be plagues and sickness; it occurs to me how they may even want to kill one another to get that meat protein they so much believe in.

If we could understand what is happening to our bodies in a low calorie or famine state, as nature begins her housecleaning, it could save many lives through the trials to come. It could even help people who say on Fast Sunday, "I just cannot fast two meals, because I get such a sick headache."

A certain chemist gives this definition in agreement with Joseph Smith:

"Some biologists hold the view that there is an intimate molecule of building up and the breaking down. The question may be asked, do not the particles that compose man's body, when they return to mother earth, go to make or compose other bodies? No, they do not. Some philosophers have asserted the human body changes every seven years. This is not correct, for it never changes. That is, the substances of which it is composed do not pass off and other particles of matter come to take their places. Neither can the particles which have composed the body of man, become a part of the bodies of other men, beasts, fowl, fish, insects or vegetables. They are governed by divine law, and though they may pass from the knowledge of the scientific world, that Divine law still holds and governs and controls them."

65

Joseph Smith states in the Documentary History of the Church, Volume 5,

"There is no fundamental principle belonging to the human system, that ever goes into another in this world or in the world to come. I care not what the theories of men are. We have the testimony that God will raise us up and he has the power to do it. If anyone supposes that any part of our bodies that is the fundamental part thereof ever goes into another body, he is mistaken."

What about the protein theory? Aren't you glad to know that piece of chicken or that pig you ate has not become a fundamental part of your body or your arm or leg? These foods we eat are only fuel. If it were otherwise we would never grow old and scars would disappear. Many wrong assumptions have been taught in the schools of health. The microscope even appears to prove the error, noting that as the tissue repairs it shows that the condition of the blood is characterized by fewer white cells. To me this would mean that the toxic waste, or white cells, had not as yet moved out into the blood, releasing the body of waste, allowing it again to heal to a normal function. You can take a person who has a slow-healing skin condition or pimples and put them on a fast of either straight water or fruit, and the white count increases to almost leukemia proportions, depending on how encumbered with waste the body is and how much or how fast waste moves out into the blood; and quickly the pimples or skin condition heals.

After two years of strict fruit diet and periodic fasting, Professor Ehret said, on healing wounds,

> "With a knife I made an incision in my lower arm; there was no flow of blood as it thickened instantly; closing up the wound, no inflammation, no pain, no mucus and pus; healed up in three days, blood crust thrown off. Later, with vegetaric food, including mucus-ferments (starch food), but without eggs and milk, the wound bled a little, caused some pain and pussed slightly, a light inflammation, complete healing only after some time. After the same wounding, with meat-food and some alcohol; longer bleeding, the blood of a light color, red and thin, inflammation, pain, pussing for several days, and healing only after a two days' fasting."

It has been my experience that this is true. With delivery of the baby I had during my two years' fruit diet, I had no pain and no bleeding.

What appears to be a blood cell (red) is different varieties of fuel food in process of change or combustion into energy. These would depend on the type of food ingested. The microscope has brought with it many misconceptions. Once off on this track into misconception and incorrect assumption, the truth is lost in a maze of color and type of food pattern which we label the blood cell. These are thought to build and break down every few seconds and make new ones. It has brought with it some interesting and helpful ideas, however. Bacteria, poisons, metals, etc., have been identified. Knowing what poison you are dying of, if an antidote is known, is certainly helpful. The idea that the body is changing into renewed cells at the rate of 300,000 new cells every second is incorrect, and it is this error which takes us further into the fairy tale, not realizing the kind of fuel we really need for best results in health, performance and long life. We place in our stomachs whatever is at hand or is pleasing to the palate and in whatever mixtures, with never a thought as to how this is all combining or to what form of gas and poison the combination may be producing, not to mention what that particular poison may be doing to our body. A research into the types of fuel (food, herbs, antidotes, poisons, etc.) is the thing we need now — and less time and money spent on chasing rainbows and trying to find the elusive pot of gold at the end of the chase into the wrong concepts. Man is ever learning but never coming to a knowledge of the truth. Men of learning in our day may never allow themselves the luxury of knowing anything for sure. When the puzzle medical science is trying to construct uses, as its foundation, such gross errors, it is understandable why the men of scholarly report must base their knowledge on such a wishy-washy premise that there are no absolutes. So on we stumble down the wrong path with the sophistication of modern man, deluded with the idea that anything newly written will certainly be obsolete within a short time; so we set it aside with a sigh and choose to live in the present fickle trend of fashions of the learned, while missing many of the wonderful truths that men of wisdom have known through all the dispensation of time on the earth. Taking the wrong path, we miss the destination of light where truth and wisdom dwell.

This compares with the world's concept of the Godhead; as long as man does not understand what or who it is that he worships, he can only worship fable, a myth, a false God. He might as well worship the golden calf. Not being acquainted with the true God, he lives with little half truths, and these half truths lead him off in the wrong direction where the incorrect conclusions are drawn. The geologist has done the same thing, made an incorrect assumption because he did not know, or did not listen to the word of the Lord, giving the answer as to the length of time the earth has existed. Had he listened, he may have saved a lot of time. He could have (like an algebra problem) known the answer in the first place, then spent his time in research to find out why the answer was correct, in the end proving it to himself and to the world, as the problem came with all of its answers to the correct conclusion, the same answer that God gave in the first place.

Mankind stumbles along in his puffed-up knowledge, not recognizing that all the answers, like the algebra problem, God gives to anyone who asks; and he even gives the follow-up reasons why it is so, if anyone will take the trouble to ask in faith. It may take a lifetime to find out why, and for the most part it does; but if enough faith were exhibited, learning could be sped up to a rate we in our fallen state could hardly comprehend. The first thing we teach our children, as soon as they are able to learn anything, is the true meaning of the Godhead, and how to contact that source of all truth. Our child learns in his infancy a truth which kings, rulers, great statesmen, and scientists do not know. He learns who God is, his relationship to Jesus Christ and to the Holy Ghost; and we also teach him how to tap into that great source of all knowledge and truth, with prayer. Then we send him on to various church auxiliary meetings to prove the answers he has already received. As he recognizes the answers as they come to him, we call this testimony. Then when all of the pieces to the puzzle are placed together in their proper places, we call this knowledge. All this we do on faith, believing that God knows the answer. We set out on the interesting journey of life to learn why it is so, to share with God the knowledge of the universe, ourselves, each other and all the whys and the hows that fill the immensity of time and space. What a wonderful way to learn, being led on by the spirit of God, always trusting in His first answers; recognizing, as the pieces fit into place; then pursuing the problem to a perfect knowledge.

All things can be learned this way, but we often choose to go our own way, wasting our time in fables, half truths, and puff up our chests in the belief that we are all-wise, when our wisdom is foolishness with God — "When they are learned they think they are wise." We often even argue with every new truth that He gives to the man who is willing to listen to the answer. All of the great inventions have had to surmount almost the travail of childbirth to finally get past the learned man who thinks he knows.

The entire misconcept of body metabolism has led us into drugs, unnecessary surgery, incorrect diet, inability to overcome disease, thus compounding disease of a chronic nature and causing a sickness of a world which totters under the weight of hospital bills, doctor bills, the mentally ill, the sickness of loved ones, the retarded, the expense of prisons and houses for the mentally ill (where they can be "rehabilitated") or an institution to care for the needs of those unwanted, old, or physically undesirable.

68

Brigham Young said,
Journal of Discourses 15:225:

> *"Doctors make experiments, and if they find a medicine that will have the desired effect on one person, they set it down that it is good for everybody, but it is not so, for upon the second person that medicine is administered to, seemingly with the same disease, it might produce death. If you do not know this, you have not had the experience that I have. I say that unless a man or woman who administers medicine to assist the human system to overcome disease, understands, and has that intuitive knowledge, by the Spirit, that such an article is good for that individual at that very time, they had better let him alone. Let the sick do without eating, take a little of something to cleanse*

the stomach, bowels and blood, and wait patiently, and let nature have time to gain the advantage over the disease.

If we live as the Lord intended us to live, walking with our hands in His, learning by the Spirit about those foods or herbs necessary for our well-being, then when we are in deep error and become sick, by faith we can go to His Priesthood delegates to be healed. Brigham Young, Journal of Discourses:

> *"Instead of calling for a doctor you should administer to them by the laying on of hands and anointing of oil, and give them mild food, and herbs, and medicines that you understand; and if you want the mind and will of God at such a time, get it, it is just as much your privilege as of any other member of the Church and Kingdom of God."*

Too much time is spent as a result of the lack of faith, in learning too many things that are not true. The medical profession has used too many big words to keep the lay person in darkness and confusion. The time will come when these big words of the medical language will have to be altered to meet the needs of truth.

Moses Maimonides made an interesting observation about the receiving of light and truth; this is so without the Gift of the Holy Ghost:

> *"Do not imagine that these most difficult problems can be thoroughly understood by any one of us. This is not the case. At times a truth shines so brilliantly that we perceive it as a clear day. Our nature and habit then draws a veil over our perception and we return to a darkness almost as dense as before. We are like those who, though beholding frequent flashes of lightning, still find themselves in the thickest darkness of the night."*

What is needed in order that man may live out his days in happiness, is a change in the path, back to the correct concept of body metabolism. Let him clean the blood of debris, feed himself the correct fuel and man will live to the age of a tree; and Christ will come and dwell with him for a thousand years of peace and happiness, and he will be able to tolerate the presence of the Lord, because he will be clean and pure physically and spiritually, giving perfect obedience to the law upon which his physical body was created.

CHAPTER THREE

COLOR, SOUND AND THE AURA
CHOICE VS. CONDITIONED REFLEX

We hear a lot lately in the sale of stereo equipment of a connection between color and sound, but how many of you have seen the colors of musical sound? There are colors that can be seen and felt in different sound vibrations. Music can be an aid to health and happiness. Music can also aid in the healing process.

Of late we have produced too many inharmonious sounds, and some of the young have inflicted them upon each other to cause even torment, chaos, and sickness. Tests have been made in hot houses using hard rock music on some plants and beautiful, harmonious music on others. The plants receiving beautiful music grew healthily, while the loud music caused the other plants to wither and die.

Much of the illness we observe can be attributed to the kind of sound color vibrations we hear around us. Much of the music we listen to is heard only because it is on the radio. Then as we become more and more nervously upset, we finally snap it off. Sometimes we listen to the music, advertising and talk sounds of the disc jockey, never realizing it is all contributing to our ill health. There are some who cannot go for a moment without the clatter of sound around them. The noise serves as a buffer against the intolerable sounds of silence, becoming almost an addiction stirred by such passion, they create a permanent sense of excitement. Intense anxiety is the result. Loud music sound is one of the genuine causes for social tension.

Some of the youngsters who have taken drugs have seen the colors of sound vividly and have tried to reproduce them in the psychedelic colors and the strobe light, using both in rhythm with the excitable colors of the bizarre sounds that drain their physical bodies of vitality. Then using the drugs that weaken, along with the lack of nourishing food, it ultimately brings with it the stimulation to sexual violation, perversion, and venereal disease.

We see drooping shoulders, sick, unkempt hair, the dull and lifeless skin of a sick 70-year-old wrapped around the teenager, who lays hopelessly around the park trying to find peace from the confused world he has created for himself, blaming his elders for causing the mess the world is in, thus creating the gap that destroys an intimate happy family atmosphere.

We have allowed the satanic sounds of the African drum beating to the pulse of our hearts, ever throbbing, pound our lives into a frenzy, allowing Satan to take possession of our souls.

Even the war drums of the American Indian do not have the driving force of the hard rock music of today. At first the garbled sounds of the new psychedelic music covered the shock of the deeper motive, which desired to match the frenzy of the music to the perversion of vulgar words. Later on, however, as people became used to these tainted phrases, the musicians brought their sounds into clearer focus, exposing the now acceptable vulgarity unashamedly naked to our ears. Pope said,

> "Vice is a monster of such horrid mien,
> As to be hated, needs but to be seen;
> Yet seen too oft, familiar
> With her face
> We first endure, then pity, then embrace."

We become so used to these sounds we almost link them to progress.

All that modern Israel would have to do to undermine the beauty and vigor of their Sabra youth would be to allow the satanic beat of hard rock to invade their places of amusement. It looks as though the Jews are smarter than that. Their young people are the backbone of their nation — and they seem to know it. Maybe they have observed the deterioration in the backbone of America.

The sights and sounds of the drug trip are phony, a counterfeit given of evil, showing often, all in one overwhelming whack, some truths it takes a lifetime of spiritual living to arrive at. This would be Satan's way, as too much knowledge, even truth, that cannot be accepted can destroy;

the correct way would be: truth upon truth, knowledge upon knowledge, until we come to a perfect knowledge.

Many young people have gone completely insane from taking L.S.D. The ones who seem to survive it the best are those who have had some spiritual training at home. Many who have survived mentally and realized it was wrong are seeking spiritual experiences among the occult religions, and still others are able to come back to Christianity.

Since the intensity of war has subsided somewhat, music sounds have settled to a little different beat — more love songs and a little less agony. With the drug trip, young people thought they had had a spiritual experience their parents knew nothing about. The true and genuine spiritual experiences, that these flower children know nothing about, can only be received on the principles of righteousness. You cannot break God's laws or morality, dissipating and destroying the temple housing the soul, and say you have had a spiritual, heavenly experience in the process.

When obedience to God's laws and righteousness prevail, then will the soul drink deeply, seeing and feeling the colors of sound vibrations. There have been tests made by blind people (not blind from birth) who each verify certain notes as having a certain color.

When you look at the clothes draped in a pioneer museum, the drab colors — blacks, browns, and some whites — you are suddenly aware of the vast color variety that surrounds our lives today. We have learned that color becomes a rich addition to the learning process. When the colors are jumbled together, without harmony in their relationships to one another, the mind becomes confused and an agitation is set in motion — even if you have no knowledge of color combinations — the same way it affects you to have someone banging at random on a piano.

You can walk into a room that is beautifully and harmoniously decorated, whether it is done in brilliant, stimulating colors or quiet, restful colors and say, "This is really beautiful, isn't it," even though you may not know why or how the decorator achieved such beauty and form. There are sound colors that are stimulating to the physical: happy, melancholy, depressing; stimulating to the intellect; stimulating to the spiritual: restful, peaceful, heavenly; sleep music; sounds to read by; or agitating sounds; there are also spooky sounds that set up vibrations of fear or impending disaster.

With the eight notes of music we use, there are endless variations for all moments and moods. We certainly have not found them all, so there is no reason for us to be inflicted with the monotony of a "Johnny One Note." Out of the period in history where there were terrible plagues and intense suffering came some of the truly classical sounds in harmony that had not been previously known in world history.

Along with the beauty in the music of the masters came some very depressing sounds in classical music. Out of the young peoples' pain with drugs have come many distortions in negative sounds; but along with these negative sounds has come also a new music with some very interesting variations in positive sound and harmony that will have an effect on many generations to come. All beautiful works of art, be it music, art, or literature, have been born of great discipline, joy or suffering.

Some music can stimulate to motion, as in dancing, some to a frenzy. We have music to go to war by, music that can welcome home from war. There is much happy and stimulating music. Young people like the rhythmic sounds of happiness; with a feeling of nostalgia, the older people are made young momentarily when they fill that moment with young sounds.

We need all types of positive sounds to make our lives complete. The negative sounds are those that destroy the body and mind. It is so often a difficult problem for youngsters who try hard to be acceptable to their social groups when the choices in sound related to their contemporary world become distorted enough to kill their physical bodies. If we could learn to move easily from one vibration of positive sound to the other, our lives would play a gentle song always in our hearts. We could use each sound to enhance the moment's need, whether to stimulate for work or play, to lift to heavenly spheres, to relax from cares of the world, or whatever your life pattern may need at that time. This is an art in and of itself, and few people find it. It is like the man who plays dreamy, relaxing music while driving and falls asleep at the wheel. It is like playing the right song with the right movie. Too often we use all the wrong song and to excess.

Once while doing dishes at my grandmother's and whistling a song as I worked, she chided me, saying, "You will never get those dishes done if you don't whistle something more lively." When you begin to look for harmony in your being, you may be thrillingly surprised to see the beautiful colors of sound.

In the last 60 years or so, we have been bombarded with a spectacle of fabulous color. That it has aided in education is well known, but what about all of the doses of jumbled, inharmonious color we get each day in the supermarket? The walls and floors may be in harmony, but what about the maze of colored boxes and packages that stare at us, like a crazy patchwork quilt, from the shelves and display racks?

Experts in color, and there are as many as there are experts in the effects of color sound, know which colors you will pick up and which ones will sell their products. Each box and package has been well planned by color combinations, coupled with advertising to assist you in your choice. This may be all well and good, but when it is all under one roof and lumped into this mass of color, it becomes a drain on the body, a psychedelic confusion to the mind. People who are very sick, or extremely sensitive, have a hard time with the supermarket. The fruit and vegetables market has a much better effect, as you move from one beautiful color to another in an order; and the most successful fruit markets are those that learn to display their wares in the harmony of the color chart. You may say this sort of thing is all around us in everything. True, and the most difficult is in the city where the jumble blasts at you from all sides, adding its lights of color to the color vibrations of sound.

74 It has been said by many experts of late that stress is the cause of the world's troubles. Much of the stress we have to cope with today is caused by color and sound. Our ancestors had war, famine, plague, fear, taxes, and all the rest; but the things we have that they did not are the colors, sounds, chemical food, fallouts, poor air, poor water, and speed. These give us the advantage in stress. Do you expect that I will say to get rid of the colors? When the hippies went to the psychedelic colors in sight and sound, they also soon went to drab clothes and makeup and headed for the open road to find peace in between the noisy times they made their music.

The body can only stand so much that is not in harmony. Where colors are concerned, it can only stand so much of the colors that stimulate, the way it can only stand so many hours of work, and then it must rest. It has been said that we must slow down. Personally I see nothing wrong with the progress we have made in transportation (except for the smog that it has created). The high speed on the open road or high speed in an airplane do not compare to the high speed racing around among all the psychedelic color and noise of a city, where stress is concerned, unless, of course, you are afraid to fly.

That you can get used to it is possibly true, but can you be sure that it does not effect you healthwise?

Dante said,

> "Art, as far as it is able, follows nature as a pupil imitates his master, thus your art must be, as it were, God's grandchild."

The art that has become popular, adding its sick aura to an already sick society is the horror of modern art.

If the love of expressing inner feelings and sharing them with others becomes strong enough, this powerful aura develops a master. As expressed by Millet,

> "Oh how I wish I could make those who see my work, feel the splendor and terrors of the night! One ought to make people hear songs, the silences of murmurings of air. They should feel the infinite."

Think for a moment about the colors that God uses the most, and think about the effect these colors have on you. Different colors have a positive or negative effect; the greens are restful, peaceful colors; the fields and the trees. When we get into the muddy green, however, these are the sick colors, the colors of nausea, and they have an adverse effect on us. Too many people, led by the fashions of the day, have carpeted their floors with the negative colors of nausea and wonder why they do not feel well. These are the people who head for the hills each chance they get to be away from home. Sometimes people carpet their floors with the stimulating color in the reds which when lived with too much provokes to anger or short temper.

75

One time a real estate man was helping me to find a house. As we drove up to a lovely home he said, "So sad these people are getting a divorce, and have several children." When I walked into the house I felt that I knew one of the reasons. The entire house was done in red. Now days peoples' homes are a place to escape, rather than a heaven on earth, and a refuge from the terror and turmoil around them. It is important to surround yourself, in your home, with the colors that rest you from the cares of the world; but it is also important not to make it such a restful place that you do not ever want to leave it to face the outside. There should be some stimulating colors. You can change your clothing colors to suit your mood also. When we are young we like the more exciting, stimulating colors. We see the bright, gay colors filling the nursery.

These colors are correct and educational for children, but remember, too much can confuse and hamper them. As we mature and mellow (if we do), we tend to wear quiet, pastel colors.

The light blues are the reflected colors of heaven that fill us with "awe" and the love of God and a knowledge of eternity, as the blues and whites spread across the immensity of time and space, speaking always tenderly to us of peace and hope.

Brown has a touch of most colors — with the brown of trees, earth, and rocks, God has tempered its somber color with the greens. Too much brown can be drab and sad. The woman who becomes a little "brown bird" does herself an injustice. When she changes to the softness of pink, she will attract more love. When she changes to the brighter colors, she will stimulate more interest. Men have for too long thought it feminine for them to dress with color. It is a pleasant change to the eyes of women to see their men dressed in something other than drab blacks and browns.

Purple is the color of royalty, a color of wealth and progress; but, like red, it can be too stimulating when too much is used. Softening it to the lavenders brings quiet spirituality.

Black is the absence of all color and is associated with evil and darkness. Its somber color is morbid and unhappy unless used as an outline and in association with other colors. They are even making blackboards now of cream white and using bright blue and other colored chalk. Hospital rooms have become softly colorful, as the experts have learned more and more about the importance of color in healing the sick. The experts have also learned that the classroom colors aid or retard the learning process. Is it not time that we as mothers begin to become expert in this business of color so as to help our families find a little piece of heaven on earth — a place to come home to for consolation rather than a place from which to run?

There could be many volumes written about color, and it is not my intention to cover the subject extensively here. It is helpful to know a little about the colors we can and do reflect from our bodies to the people around us, so I will place more emphasis on the aura.

The Russians have done a great deal of research on the aura of color and light which surrounds the human body. Photographs have been made of it. The first time I learned about the aura was from a little book of suggestions for missionaries. All good salesmen and missionaries knowlingly or unknowingly learn to reflect the correct color in order to make a sale or a convert.

There is an aura, or we will call it an intangible reflection, given off by each person at all times. This aura changes color as moods change, and those around feel or see the color subconsciously, at times consciously. Joseph Smith in his vision of God the Father and His Son Jesus Christ described their light and the beauty of their aura as being brighter than the noonday sun. All artists in history describe the aura as a "halo" of light around the heads of saints and angels.

In our fallen state few people ever achieve a brilliance of aura enough to make a light around them, yet the Lord has commanded us to: Matthew 5:16:

> "Let your light so shine before men, that they may see your good works, and glorify your Father which is in heaven."

In order for the salesman or the missionary to be successful, he must radiate the brilliance of enthusiasm, yellows and golds. When the enthusiasm becomes very intense, it begins to spark off gold and silver; and soon the yellows, golds, and silvers become so intense as to glow almost white. As these sparks fly off one person, they electrically attach themselves somehow to people around them; and other people will begin to sparkle with the same feeling of enthusiasm. When the light of a heavenly spirit is pulsing through this enthusiastic person, people around are generated to the joy of "awe" and are brought to tears. This happens with great art, great literature, and great music. Certain words, certain works of art maintain an aura around them that is timeless. Anything that has gone out to the world to touch men's souls generation after generation was bought only with discipline and repentant purity at its conception.

Leonardo da Vinci said,

> "If thou wouldst be an artist, forsake all sadness and care; save for thy art. Let thy soul be as a mirror which reflects all objects, all movement and color, remaining itself unmoved and clear."

There are certain words and combinations of words relating to sounds considered unclean by heaven, which fall from our tongues, and when spoken have a negative force about them. It has been said that the Hebrew language is the nearest to the pure language of heaven. Zwingli said of Hebrew as he was learning the language,

"I found the Holy Tongue beyond all belief cultivated graceful and dignified. Although poor in the number of words, yet its lack is not felt, because it makes use of its store in so manifold a fashion; indeed I may dare to say that if one conceives its dignity and grace, no other language expresses so much with so few words, and so powerful expressions. No language is so many-sided with meaningful modes of imagery – no language so delights and quickens the human heart."

Though we may not know the errors of sound words attached to evils of the past, there are many things we say from day to day which, when sent forth from our tongues, cause us to be ill and have a negative effect on our aura; for example, "That just kills me," "My aching back," "He gives me a pain in the neck," "I wish I were dead," "Scared to death," "I felt like knocking his head off." At a ballgame they yell, "Kill him," "I could kill you," not to mention the cursings people use in the name of heaven or hell. Thoughts are things; sounds are things; colors are things—words are things. The prayers that rise heavenward are things. The Lord gave us a pattern for prayer in "The Lord's Prayer," and it would not surprise me if it had a special significance in its pattern of words that makes a direct quick connection to heaven's realm.

78

All of the things we think, say, do, or surround ourselves with are the sum total of the colors in the aura we expel to those around us. At times it may be beautiful, at times negative and ugly.

The muddy green is the aura of sickness and is repellant to everyone. This is why so few people can stand to nurse or doctor the sick. Remaining around the negative sick can suck you in, the same way the positive colors' sparkle of silver or gold can be communicated from one person to another. Often people who tend the needs of the sick become hardened and cross, almost unfeeling in their detached, impersonal attention, because they must build a wall of resistance or go under with their patients. The person whose aura does not lift, sparkle and, by love, with its own beauty, help the sick, has no business in the profession. It is like having an elementary school teacher who hates children. The profession alone, as being a leader of men, should develop character and selfless love. Since there are so many sick and so few with this kind of aura, it becomes a burdensome task to care for the sick, with only the rewards of the weekly paycheck.

The colors of anger can also be felt and seen to the extent that you have all heard, "I saw red," or "red with anger." The colors of jealousy are certain shades of green, mixed with shades of dark red, black, and brown, adding green color to the face that has been noted as "green with envy." Certain shades of blue, mixed with grey, have also been noted in connection with sadness and despair, "She is blue today."

Listed will be some of the main colors it is said that we radiate. If we could see or perceive all of these colors immediately, we could recognize error more quickly and either leave the negative and walk away or do something to help. Often, not being aware, we are all mixed up in the ball of snakes before we know what has happened. We are told not to judge people, and seeing the aura may cause us to judge. We should be able to make a judgment of evil or good in people, circumstances, etc., enough to know whether or not to become involved, as with marriage, business, and friends. Since we are not all smart enough at all times, we have the wonderful gift of the spirit to depend on if we are willing to listen.

clear blue .... high spirituality
blue with lavender ....,.... high idealism
   blue with dark reddish brown .... selfish religions
   blue with grey .... religious fear, despair, sad
   blue with black .... superstitious religion
   lavender .... high spirituality
   violet .... spiritual dedication
   orchid .... perception
   pure yellow .... spiritual intellect
   sparkle of gold and silver .... enthusiasm
   orange .... intellect (intellectual study)
   orange with brick red .... low mental cunning
   light green .... sympathy and understanding
   medium green .... adaptable
   green with red, brown, dark red, black .... jealousy
   green with grey.................................. deceit
   pure carmine (rose color) .... love, human affection
   scarlet .... self pride and will
   bright brick red .... anger, color of dead blood
   bright red .... excitement-stimulant color
                                        of good blood

79

The aura changes like the kaleidoscope with our moods. Perhaps if we knew others were feeling or seeing these things, it would help us to cultivate positive attitudes and beautiful auras. Once when I was lecturing to a group of people and talking about the aura, a woman in the audience said, "I can see your aura, it's gold and light green. What does that mean?" I was stunned for a moment as my aura was to be bared to the group till I realized that was not so bad. If we can begin to develop a peaceful, beautiful, cheerful, loving attitude, we will not only have a lovely aura, but we will also have health.

The aura about each of us touches a sensitive chord of human feeling. Those who live in a negative aura pick up more readily the negative vibrations of other negative people, as in mob violence or argument. Those who live in a positive aura of spirit by faith with love and peace pick up quickly those same vibrations and repel the negative, seeking only the good vibrations such as are felt in church and called the spirit of the meeting. Those who are too sensitive of self pick up vibrations easily from both sides and are torn. To be selfishly sensitive is a route to pain. If sensitivity lives with self long enough to know how others feel and long enough to generate an innate empathy, then can we lift and help ourselves as well as others. Strength of character and aura come only from lifting, not ever from leaning. The next thing indispensable to a beauty of the spirit is a desire to learn the laws of God and obey them. With true obedience followed by its rewarding blessings comes confidence and understanding, and from this, springs great love of God, self, and others.

If our vibrations are changing from positive to negative in rapid succession, we develop in our lives the confusion and pain of psychedelic color. The people who live the most with this kind of good and bad are those who want to do wrong but know they should not. They are they who **know** better than they **do,** who continue to put the hand on the flame, knowing they will be burned but have not the character to resist. We all fall into this pit at times. Repentance is a marvelous principle. The cleaner the body, the more beautiful and sparkling the aura becomes, and the more easily it changes in color from one positive mood to another. The purer the spirit, the more beautiful, radiant light surrounds the person, enabling him to resist the negative forces around him. We have discussed cleansing the body. In order to develop the spirit so that its light will shine, one must overcome fear. Fear is the great destroyer of the soul. To live with fear is to bring upon oneself the negative things one fears. There are people who enjoy pain and suffering and do all they can to hold it to themselves. They enjoy telling others about their misfortunes, seeking nothing but the rewards of sympathy. There are those also who enjoy fear, making it a part of them, clinging to it tightly as if it had virtue. These are the people who spread a muddy green aura like a plague around them, repelling the very people whose approval and sympathy they seek. Without faith we cannot please God.

Gibby said,

"Worry and Faith are bitter enemies; when Worry enters, Faith goes out the back door."

and

"Security is not born of inexhaustible wealth, but of unquenchable faith."

It requires faith in our tomorrows to have health and beauty of spirit.

Thinking about and attempting to convey to you some of the things contributing to or detracting from health and our aura, I must touch on at least one of the things we live with in a modern society which causes illness. I could write of the daily agitations driving on the freeway, in places of entertainment, restaurants, hotels, beauty shops, barber shops, garages, the way we earn our living in general, the weary housewife, not to mention the debts we owe or the things that break down and have to be fixed — the irritations in our general communication with other people. This is not given in a negative way but rather to help you to become aware of some of the causes of poor aura vibrations, as well as sickness. There is nothing personal in my statement toward any particular store.

81

Have you ever walked into a large discount-type department store and felt the vibrations of bizarre noise and clamor and wondered what the difference was in an expensive store where things are more harmoniously displayed and people more relaxed, soft music playing? Did you ever wish you didn't have to shop at a discount store again? If you ever noticed or felt this, you are a more sensitive and spiritual person. The reasons for the differences are simple.

In the discount store, things on the shelves move quickly because more people live in the inexpensive bracket; consequently, the hubbub of display and rack change. No time for particular beauty or harmony, the low cost will sell the product. No need to fuss. The help is underpaid, no need to hire decorators at a better wage. Price reductions will sell the product. The result is inharmony in color and display.

The people who shop are usually in a hurry because many need that dress or whatever to wear tomorrow and didn't get paid until today.

They really cannot afford to buy the article, but it is a necessity, so the feeling of worry surrounds their aura like a somber black shroud.

Then there are those who have saved a little and realize if they are ever to get ahead, they must buy at bargain prices and they stalk the store with a feeling of superiority, knowing they have a few extra dollars to spend on some bargain, just waiting to pounce on it when it comes their way. Often they buy something they neither needed nor wanted, but they take pride on their ability to find a bargain and to have enough in the purse to pay for it when it comes by. In making the exchange from money to product, they smugly leave the premises.

Others, however, after finding the coveted bargain, too quickly grab it up and after surrendering money from pocket to clerk, feel a sense of remorse for bad judgment and doubts and fears of not being able to acquire more money to fill the pocket again. They spread their aura with dense darkness which occupies the surrounding area several feet out from their bodies with gloom and darkness.

Then there are those who forgot a tool or need a tire or some important food or clothing item in order to go on the next day. Some run the gauntlet of many stores in search of the needed item, not finding it, and with each store panic grows and the vibrations they expel from their bodies by anger, frustration, disappointment, and panic is a pain to all who come within their range.

There are those who take tired little children for a nice relaxing evening to the local discount store in the hope of a little change from staying home all day or working at a dull job. They do not have anything in particular to shop for; they only need a night out and cannot afford anything else so, not being able to afford a baby sitter, they drag tired little junior with up-lifted arm into the maze of color and noise and confusion and poor vibrations which make up the local discount store. Pretty soon, said family begins to pick up all these poor vibrations and junior, being the most sensitive and tired, begins to bawl. Dad, being a strong masculine type who would like to think he can solve all problems, suddenly feels the hopelessness of the whole situation and his automatic reaction is anger. So he adds his poor vibrations to the general atmosphere of said store and leaves in a huff. All family members are exhausted and angered and tainted by the smear of bad color vibrations and feelings.

Then there are the clerks of the discount store who live day after day in this overwhelming array of horrid vibrations and, not being able to help themselves, become a party to the problem.

Your clerk is weary and wishes you would go home and never come back, and with a plastic smile and a look of bitterness in her eye, she extends to you the immensely original and heartwarming salute, "Thank you for shopping at so and so."

Then there is the loud blare of the intercom as the lady with the squally voice screeches, "Attention discount shoppers, for the next five minutes we will be running a special in the men's and boys' underwear department. Boxers and t-shirts will be on sale for one-half price. Get 'em while they last," and she concludes with the familiar words the discount shopper grows to hate the most, "Thank you for shopping at so and so."

Then the excitement swells and all who want to join in the fun make a mad dash for the men's and boys' underwear department. As the items are snatched from customer to customer, the vibrations of hate and envy build to an almost explosive crescendo.

Then there are the dressing rooms in the discount store where, if you have not picked up the already existing bad vibrations around you, at this point you can usually manufacture your own. When the guard of the dressing room gives you your allotted number of garments and locks the chain behind you, making you feel like a common criminal, you proceed to your assigned three by three cell. The annoyance begins as you try to close the curtains which are extremely inadequate to cover the opening. Then the struggle begins in this ridiculously small area. Between trying to dress, keeping your backside from being exposed to the public, and keeping the clothes up off the grimy floor, your patience has somehow expired and your aura has changed to a luscious brick shade of red, adding its fire to the sickening air of the entire store.

When upon arrival at the checkstand you find to your confused amazement two lines of what appears to you to be dozens of people each, waiting, while the ten other checkstands are chained in idleness. After becoming increasingly impatient, you have almost arrived at the point of debarkation, and you've nearly escaped this madness, when you find that you've left your purse in the dressing room, or the clerk says with a shrug of indifference to the only person barring your escape. "Do you remember the price on this?" His negative answer causes her to send a slow stockroom boy to the far corner of the store for a price check.

After we emerge from this dark background into the fresh air and the frenzy begins to subside, we soon forget. There are many little and big agitations which we develop ourselves, but there are many which surround us in crowded places, tainting and touching our lives. But for some unknown reason, we always go next payday and do it all again.

The other type of store, the expensive store, has an entirely different atmosphere, for the most part.

Mr. and Mrs. Shopper have enough money to spend; the thought doesn't often occur to them to worry about it. They vaguely keep their spending in hand. They know there is more where that came from. Often they buy items ahead of their needs on sale, like sheets, etc., so they always have an abundance at home. They grocery shop the same way. Their shelves are full at all times, so no need to rush around. They shop, at times, just for the relaxa tion and pleasure of seeing lovely new things, where colors and music play a sort of harmony on the soul. Even in this lovely atmosphere, there are some bad vibrations. The clerks often radiate a poor vibration. If they are working at a low wage for a living, their worry and frustration is evident, here, surrounded with all this loveliness, and not being able to taste a single bit.

Expensive stores usually hire mature women who need something to do to occupy their time since children have gone. Some of these women have usually been surrounded with all the luxuries they have gathered around them all their lives. Her husband still supports her, and any money she makes, she can put on her back so she can look nice for the public; and having done so, she feels happy and relaxed. She has a sense of independence and knows if husband does not want to spend his money on certain of the beautiful things she sells, she can buy them herself.

There is another type who brings bad vibrations to expensive stores, and these are the people who cannot buy but like to look awhile. They are sometimes the dreamers and wishers who spread their wishy-washy vibrations like a plague.

Then there is one other type of vibration, sometimes negative and sometimes positive. The clerk who has to work to take care of children whose father has either deserted or died, or the clerk who has to work to send a boy on a mission or a child through college. She has enough to do to keep her busy at home, and when at home she goes a hundred miles an hour to get all things done and taken care of. She usually has to sit up nights sewing for herself and her children in order to keep them and herself presentable. She is already tired when she starts to work, and it does not ever seem to get any better. The only thing that helps her vibrations at all is that she has a courageous cause and a love to express by the devoted day-after-day giving.

Another type is the person who brings an aura of bitterness with him to the expensive store, a feeling of hate and a **why**: why does someone else get to have all these nice things and he can't even have one of them.

There are those whose lives are unhappy and who look at all the pretty things. Beauty brings them some happiness and escape from the reality at home, so they relax and enjoy every minute of shopping.

Then there are those who shop just to spend time for want of something better to do to occupy their day. What a waste, and what a drain on the body.

Shopping is, at best, even in the most pleasant surroundings, poor entertainment and a waste of time. The people who develop a strength of aura help themselves by staying out of places which tend to harbor poor vibrations. The general atmosphere of human suffering which goes on during the process we call shopping is a crime against the quiet, peaceful spirit.

85

Many of our health problems are related to the acquisition of creditable achievement. When our opinion of ourselves is too low, it is difficult for our health to remain intact. So we find excuse in the new ideas that parents or circumstances are at fault. The new idea tells us that if we were brainwashed or hypnotized, we would suddenly emerge from the awful creature we have come to hate to become a solid citizen with the grandest attirbutes of integrity. Because these concepts are detrimental to the healing process, I feel it is important to mention here a word about choice versus conditioned reflex.

Since today's world has had to cope with a deluge of psychiatry and psychology, along with the fascinating new science the Russians have dubbed brainwashing, or conditioned reflex, and since it is my belief that the mind, body and soul cannot become separated except at death's consummation, and to be really well is to be spiritually, physically, intellectually, and socially well, I will undertake at this point in our discussion to touch on the subject of choice. God has granted us all the privilege of choice (free agency). No one friend or foe can force you to become conditioned to anything you do not want to become part of you. Something or someone can exert a greater influence on your choices. If a bandit put a gun in your back and asked for your money, you would want, in an unwanting way, to give it to him rather than be hurt. Parents can apply this form of force to a helpful or unhelpful end.

Even if force is for a good purpose, say developing a good habit in the child, the child may rebel to the point of going in complete opposition to the ways of the parents, anything from physical cleanliness, diet, obedience, cigarettes, liquor, drugs, telling the truth, or living generally a morally clean life. If the parents taught a good moral life by example, the child may not choose to follow. If the parents taught an immoral example, the child may desire to do the opposite. Each child has the privilege of making the decision. Some children will stand all kinds of punishment rather than give up this privilege in any way. Many grown people would rather die than be told what to do, even if it is best for them. So the child asserts his own choice in all things whether to obey or whether to suffer the consequences. Then there are those few souls who know the meaning of love and who are fortunate to have parents who love them enough to correct them out of love. These remarkable few do the right things that are best for them. Then there are those who are determined to choose evil no matter what their conditioning has been to the contrary.

A psychiatrist can only help those who have a desire to change, and the doctor's help is only needed to help the person to break habits of long standing which are too deeply rooted in the subconscious to break alone. In the case of brainwashing, we will go back to the bandit and the gun or the parents who forced the child. It is of no effect as soon as the force is removed or whatever torture is involved, whether it was a bell, sound, hunger, cold, heat, spanking, a cross word, or even a hurt look in a parent's eyes. As soon as the person is free of the restriction, he will again do as he pleases.

In most cases the people of the world allow the circumstances wherein they find themselves, circumstances brought about by their own poor choices or the poor choices of influential friends, family, etc., to set the pattern of their lives and make them miserable. Since their spirit is not strong enough to rise above these influences to the point of desire to change for the better, they live out their lives in unhappiness and so on into eternal life. Always though, there is the point of choice; you may live unhappily if you choose, no one can stop you. All great things that have been done in the soul of man or in his surroundings belong to the word "desire." A child may say when he is grown that it is all the fault of his parents that he became a second-rate citizen, but this is only an excuse for the way he chose to be. If his parents taught him many good things and he went bad, the point is well proven in this alone — again the word "desire." He did what he wanted in spite of mom and dad. This kind of strong spirit could also come back to good if he chose. Having made the choice, however, to wrong, it is unlikely, unless his opinion of the need for good changes and his desire is for good. Here again the law of the universe is absolute: if he breaks the law and is battered by it for a long time, he may, in the case of brainwashing, set himself straight with the world and the law so as not to suffer physical, spiritual, or mental anguish. This is not, however, the purpose of a loving God to, by inflicting suffering, force us to choose good. He does not always punish or chasten evil at the moment it is done. Most punishment we bring upon ourselves by disobedience to a law of truth; this is automatic, such as a finger in a socket where there is current, bringing a sudden jolt. At times, like a loving parent, God may spank us for a wrong to aid us in a correct decision, but year after year he allows the sun to rise and shine on the just and the unjust. He allows food to grow and the many blessings of nature to settle lovingly on all, good and bad alike. This patience is a blessing to us all for many doctors of the mind would place a man's soul in one category or the other (good or bad) so a title could be given to each type. Life is not like this, however, with its many varying shades of half good and half bad and the fractions of many colors in between where we find ourselves in the struggle of choices. God waits us out as we pass from one shade to another, and anytime we reach out our hand to God in faith, as a child would to a parent, the Lord is willing and waiting to help direct us to a correct choice. This we call repentance, and only a desire to change can be the basis of it.

Now we come to the point of why God wants us to make the correct choice. Is it so he can control us as robots? Is it to have us and our eternal brainwashing complete and set where no more change can take place, bound eternally to his whims and wishes? Or is it to give us a real eternal life of happiness and satisfaction as any true parent wants for his child. No parent who truly loves his child wants him eternally tied to his apron strings and bound to himself. A true loving parent wants his child to be self-sufficient and able to make his own way happily and correctly and knows the only way is through correct choices. The difference between earthly parents and heavenly parents is that earthly parents cannot always advise correctly. It would follow that the more we turn to God's laws and word to find our way, the more we work at God's direction, the sooner we arrive at a state of perfection; and it is only in this state that God can set us free, knowing we will always make the correct choices. God does not want to eternally be bound to us in a responsible way. He wants us to be free and himself also. The man who has many slaves, many servants, many houses, many animals, and many children is as much a slave to them as they are to him. As long as we are helpless babes, we are God's responsibility and he is bound to us for our care and well being. When we arrive at perfection, we set God free and ourselves also, bringing joy to us both. "Man is that he might have joy."

There is also the soul-shaking moment in our lives when a grief or shock beyond our apparent spirit strength causes us to give up the struggle for correct choices, and in doing so we make a choice anyway to wallow in our self-pity and sorrow until it beats us down to the depths of ill health. The road back is a long, hard climb and will probably take far more strength of spirit than it took to cope with the grief at the time it happened. Many times there is no return from such depths of despair and death often follows.

Much of today's arthritis is the result of a sad experience which taxes the adrenal glands to the maximum where they can no longer hold up and continue the production of cortin under such stress. This in itself makes the road back very difficult. The scripture instructs us to have faith in our tomorrows, and in spite of mistakes, to go on to hope of better and sounder judgment and greater proficiency, accepting misfortunes as part of the learning process. We recognize that constant faith, patience, hope, and a philosophic attitude is the only route to perfection. People who are generally cheerful and happy are known to be the healthiest and have by far the least conflict of soul.

The correct choice is nothing more than obedience to the laws which exist in all things. We could stand all day yelling at the light switch to come on, while refusing to place a bulb in the socket; and many of us play this sort of foolish, rebellious, nonsensical game daily in our little refusals to be obedient to God's spiritual laws which are just as real as those it takes to build a house or to do a mathematical problem. Often a more scholarly man gets the idea he is smarter than God and can figure a better way of doing things, and in doing so recognizes not that God himself must obey his own law. As we walk the earth and learn to obey the small laws and become more proficient, we will find it easier to do things we now do the hard way, just as a child, while learning, is able to do the right thing but in a hard way.

Freud has promoted an idea into the very lives of the people of today's world, infiltrating television, movies, and education. By the idea of conditioned reflex, however, too many are duped into the belief that someone else, like a hypnotist, will have to shoulder the responsibility for our mistakes. The world and its problems, our homes and people who surround us may have an effect on us, but we must remember we always stand at the helm of our own ship. Let's not look to circumstances for excuses for our lack of correct choices.

There are many great and wonderful powers hidden deep in the minds of men. When the minds of men close to these hidden powers with their outward form and inner harmony, exaltation gives way to bitterness and despair.

As long as we continue to intensely seek after change by the stimulant of evil, we cannot enter entirely into the higher realm of existence. We can only step in from time to time, taking small sips, to briefly enlighten our darkened soul, for to stay long becomes painful and boring. We must fall back into the loud, bizarre world from which we emerged for a moment, the world that always leaves us dissatisfied, bored, alone, and weary. Our weary soul can only remain in the focus of the completely beautiful light of heaven — be it music, art, truth, contentment, quiet peace, serenity, or joy — momentarily. As the brightness of sunlight in the eyes becomes painful to the soul who has just wandered from darkness into the light of heaven's realm, the more we can tolerate the quiet, beautiful, serene world of heaven, while still involved in helping our fellowmen, the longer we can remain in the gentle, loving arms of the aura of heavenly things, the more perfect and Godlike we are becoming until heaven's doors will open wide to usher us in for eternity into the ever-beautiful world where God and Christ dwell. It is time to flee from self-doubt and use our energies in the pursuit of health and happiness. Obedience removes the struggle and conflict. We always stand at the "y" in the road making a choice. How will we choose? "Man is that he might have joy."

CHAPTER FOUR

ANTIDOTES — THE HERBS
AND HOME REMEDIES

If I were to go into the study of herbs extensively, you would, I am sure, not have the capacity to endure. The study is so vast it would take more than a lifetime to learn it all. There is no one way to heal disease with nature's medicines. Some herbs have remained in use almost at all times since the world began. There are a few recent works on herbs for medicine on the market, beautifully complete; and I see no reason to duplicate them here. You will find them listed in my bibliography. Instead, shown will be individual diseases or problems, giving some of the herbs useful in these cases. Having learned from personal experiences and intense study, I will present some things not taught in other herb books. There will be some few duplications when we talk of individual disease problems, but these will be given only from things I have personally experienced.

Listed also will be some formulas (herb combinations). It has been my experience that dry powdered herbs, either separate or in combination, have a superior result to herb teas, tonics, or tinctures. They are best taken in warm water, or when they may cause nausea from the bitter taste, placed in gelatin capsules.

My belief is as quoted from the Apocryphal book *The Essene Gospel of The Gospel of John:*

"*For I tell you truly, live only by the fire of life, and prepare not your foods with the fire of death, which kills your foods, your bodies and your souls also.*"

The better fuel for our bodies, as well as for medicine, would be live raw or dried foods. It appears that herbs in some magical way help to clean and clear the body of encumbered waste. Priddy Meeks in his Journal says, "Herbs have an innate intelligence." This I feel sure is true.

There are some herbs for the lungs, as with asthma, relieving the breathing within about 15 minutes, as if they went immediately to work, directing their strength to a given place in the body. Cayenne acts as a catalyst, moving herbs quickly throughout the body, especially to the head. Ginger, acting in the same capacity, spreads the herbs to the pelvis and extremities. There are herbs that will stop bleeding and herbs that do their best work on the mucus membranes. There are some that kill parasites, some that kill germs, some that heal wounds, others that take off fluid. Some relieve pain. Each one seems to know where it is assigned, and it goes about this marvelous function without the side effects of drugs.

Willard Richards and Priddy Meeks were part of the first Medical Society in Utah, when the pioneers first entered the Salt Lake Valley. Both men were herb doctors: Willard Richards would not use the harmful drugs on the market of his time, even though he had had medical training. He received a formula from Dr. Thompson for cancer. A story about Dr. Thompson is told in the book *Back to Eden* by Kloss, relative to an experience of Willard Richards'. When W. Richards stood in and assisted with an operation where his sister had a breast removed, because of his great love for her, and after watching her go through agony, he felt there must be a better way to heal cancer. On one of his many trips, as he came into a town where a crowd was dragging a man to jail, he inquired as to what the man had done; he was told that Dr. Thompson was a quack who said he could cure cancer with lobelia. He later went to the jail where Dr. Thompson was incarcerated and received permission to use his cancer formula. Remedies were, in those days, sold only under U.S. government patents. He used herbs with great success. Priddy Meeks speaks about the Thompsonian formula in his journal wih great respect. It is not known what the formula was, but I do know that there are a number of formulas today that do kill cancer and tumors, causing them to slough off.

The discovery in the Western world that acupuncture has merit is difficult for the doctors of today to accept, even when amazing healings are performed. The Chinese give an explanation they have had handed down to them for centuries; but because they either do not explain it the way it really is, or because the explanation does not fit with medical science's accepted theories, medical men try to push it off into a corner. The same thing has happened with the people who have shown them definite and positive proof of cures for cancer — and there have been many. These people with a cancer cure either wind up in jail or go to Mexico where they can be free to help cancer victims. Rather than observing the reasons why these things work and looking for the correct explanation, medical men cling bull-doggedly to their old theory of body metabolism. Or could it be they just do not want to find an answer for cancer? It costs a great deal of money to die of cancer.

The reason it has been assumed that protein is the strengthening builder is because the eating of the concentrated foods stops the process of elimination that begins as soon as you are eating only fruits and vegetables, or fasting. This process of elimination I have explained makes you feel weak at first and, not knowing what is happening to you, you immediately think you are weak from hunger. Eat the meat and feel strong again. Those people who have discovered nature's secret have found that as soon as their body is clear and clean of toxic waste, they have strength and health they have never known before. The skin softens to the beauty of a baby's. The hair shines with new luster. The eyes sparkle, and all pain is gone. Too few people have had the courage to try fasting, so it has not been popular among the mass of people, much less to try herbs.

The real secret to a beautiful body with the tone of youth lies in the kind of fuel used, along with any activity which assists nature in maintaining its ability to throw off waste — sunshine, fresh air, exercise, and good water.

Nature's herbs are medicines which assist in the removal of waste, add nourishment, and generally promote well being. The bitter herbs are in the class of medicine only to be used until the problem is solved; the mild herbs can be used as food and nourishment.

When a cancer or tumor begins to move out of the body, it will usually be expelled in mass through the nearest opening during a healing crisis. If it is in a place not near a body opening, it will gradually be picked off, a little at a time, and move the waste into the blood and out of the body. According to medical science, we are not allowed to say there is such a thing as a cure for cancer. I stand on my Constitutional rights as a citizen of the United States to have the freedom of the press to say what I have witnessed, and to testify thereto. Whether the formulas I give you will always cure cancer, I cannot say, as all do not have the vitality necessary to move the waste; but that it is possible, I have witnessed.

May I caution you as you experience the magical healing powers of herbs: do not expect them to do everything. Some people become so excited about them that they almost expect them to bring back a leg that has been cut off. There are times when the body has been damaged beyond repair.

There are many men, some of them medical doctors, who have cancer cures, who have been persecuted and now take their patients into Mexico and Europe. Many people from the United States go to them.

Some line of a poem taken from *Handbook of Medicine Regiamen Sunitatis Salernitanum* may be of interest:

"The Salerno School doth by these lines impart
All health to England's King and doth advise
From care his head to keep, from wrath his heart,
Drink not much wine, sup light and soon arise
A King that cannot rule him his diet
Will hardly rule his realm in peace and quiet –
For healthy men may cheese be wholesome food
But for the weak and sickly tis not good."

Dioscorides tells how to make a syrup of Mandrake:

MANDRAGORA SYRUP

"Boil roots in wine to a third part, and preserve the juice thus procured and give one cyathus of it to cause the insensibility of those who are to be cut or cauterised."

The Egyptians believed that mandragora was a gift to medicine from Ra, their Sun God. Mandrake was the most popular anaesthetic during the Middle Ages and on into the Elizabethan Age. As indicated in the following lines from Shakespeare, also making mention of mandrake (mandragora syrup) used to dull the senses, mandrake is used in some of the formulas listed primarily as a laxative. It only becomes a sedative when boiled.

ANTONY AND CLEOPATRA

"Give me to drink Mandragora
That I might sleep out this great gap of time
My Antony is away."

MACBETH

"Or have we eaten on the insane root
That takes the reason prisoner."

OTHELLO

"Not poppy, nor Mandragora,
Nor all the drousy syrups of the world
Shall ever medicine thee to that sweet sleep
Which thou ow'dst yesterday."

HERBAL REMEDIES

ASTHMA (hard breathing)

Lung herb, approx. 1 (oo size) cap. daily
Enema
Stop eating until breathing is normal
Approx. 1,000-2,000 mg. Vitamin C every hour
Drastic case: empty stomach using up to 1 tsp. lobelia tincture in
water
To remove cause:
Avoid upset, cats, smog, and overeating when upset
Mild food diet

94

ADDISONS DISEASE AND HYPOGLYCEMIA

Approx. 2-6 caps. licorice root powder daily
Approx. 1 tbsp. psyllium powder in glass of water or juice
Mild food diet
When colon is affected: CT-Formula, approx. 4-6 caps. daily; other-
wise CS-Formula, approx. 4-6 caps. daily
Vitamins and minerals:
Paba
Vitamin B complex
Vitamin B12
Pantothenic acid
Calcium
Niacin
Folic Acid

ARTHRITIS

Mild food diet
Approx. 1 quart carrot juice and 1 quart celery juice, raw daily, for 2
weeks, then 1 pint daily ½ carrot and ½ celery until arthritis is
gone

When adrenal is the cause, licorice
Vitamins and herbs:
  Where adrenals are involved, approx. 2 capsules licorice root
  powder daily
  Vitamin B12
  Vitamin C
  Calcium

BLADDER INFECTION

Enema and laxative herbs
Slippery elm, approx. ½ tsp. daily
Goldenseal, approx. ¼ tsp. daily
Alfalfa mint tea, approx. 1 cup every hour
Stop eating during any infection
Use fruit or fruit juice only
Goldenseal will usually stop the bleeding of the bladder with one
    application (see kidney herbs)

BURNS

Cold water until the pain stops and the area is cooled
Vitamin E oil or
Comfrey — raw, bruised, and added to small amount of water in
    blender and made into a poultice or
Aloe Vera — bruised and put directly on burn or
Powdered comfrey or goldenseal

BABY ASTHMA

Cayenne and water (weak solution) in eye dropper
Approx. 1,000 mg. Vitamin C. (see cold formula)
Approx. ½ ounce laxative tea
Enema — where fever is present
Herbs relaxing and calming to baby:
  Hops tea and honey or
  Catnip tea and honey
  To induce sleep:
  Camomile tea and honey
  NO milk — only fruit juice or alfalfa mint tea while in state of
  attack

CAYENNE HERB and some of its uses

Heart attack
Ulcers

Sore throat
Tooth ache
Wounds
Pleuresy — approx. 1 tsp. each hour
Lockjaw — combine with lobelia
High or low blood pressure
Asthma
Diptheria
Arouses all secretive organs — can be used as linament or poultice
Rapid heart
Apoplexy
Arrests gangrene
Scarlet fever
Typhoid & yellow fever
Hemorrhage
Eyes
Colds
Cold feet

CATARACTS

Equal parts goldenseal, bayberry, eye bright — approx. 3 times daily
with an eye cup, use warm water,make a strong solution, strain
through paper towel
Approx. 150 mg Vitamin B2 daily
Multiple vitamin daily

COLIC

Bayberry tea or
Alfalfa mint tea or
Ginger tea (any one, with a little honey)
No milk until attack subsides
Hot water bottle on stomach
To relax: hops tea, catnip tea or chamomile tea

COLD

Enema or laxative
Approx. 1,000 mg. Vitamin C each hour
No food, but fruit and fruit juice
Tonic teas:
    Comfrey
    Red clover
    Alfalfa mint
    Horse tail

Chest cold:
    Lung herb
    Vapor
    Mustard plaster

some cancer formulas

CANCER (Skin)

    Equal parts:
        Bees wax
        Resin
        Mutton tallow
        Oil of spike
    Heat 20 mins., cool with ½ to 1 cup of olive oil, whip and cool. Wear
        at night under bandage

CANCER FORMULAS (CS)

    Gentian — 2 parts
    Catnip — 1 part
    Bayberry bark — 1 part
    Goldenseal — 1 part
    Myrrh — 1 part
    Irish moss — 1 part
    Fenugreek seed — 1 part
    Chickweed — 1 part
    Pink root — 1 part
    Comfrey — 1 part
    Cyani flowers — ¾ part
    Bearfoot root — 1 part
    Bugleweed — 1 part
    Yellow dock — 1 part
    Prickley Ash berries — 1 part
    Pulsatillo — 1 part
    St. John's wort — 1 part
    Blue vervaine — 1 part
    Mandrake — 1 part
    Evening Primrose — 1 part
    (Approx. 6 capsules daily; later, lower to 4)

CT FORMULA 1—CANCER

    (where parasites & ulceration of colon are present)

    Cayenne — 1 part
    Black cohosh — 1 part

Saffron — 1 part
Mandrake — 2 parts
Yellow dock — 2 parts
Blue cohosh — 2 parts
Red clover — 3 parts
Comfrey — 3 parts
Blue vervaine — 2 parts
Heal all (parasites) — 2 parts
Nettle (parasites) — 2 parts
Slippery elm — 3 parts

CT FORMULA 2 — CANCER

Gentian — 2 parts
Blue vervaine — 1 part
Nettle — 1 part
Red clover — 1 part
Myrrh — 1 part
Mandrake — 2 parts
Bayberry — 1 part
Goldenseal — 1 part
Stillengia — 2 parts
Blue violet — 2 parts
Bearfoot root — 1 part
Bugleweed — 1 part
Yellow dock — 1 part
Prickley ash berries — 1 part
Pulsatillo — 1 part
St. John's wort — 1 part
(Approx. 6 capsules daily; later, lower to 4)

CANCER (what to expect)

Good and bad days
Pain when healing crisis moves waste
Approx. ¼ to ½ tsp. each lobelia and ginseng powder in water
Garlic enema with beginning of pain
Poultice of mullein — 3 parts lobelia — 1 part, put on area
Castor oil pack on liver with hot water bottle on top
Castor oil packs — soak cloth in castor oil (outing flannel, 4 thicknesses), place in plastic bag in refrigerator between treatments; place pack on affected area with heating pad or hot water bottle

CHOLERA

To kill parasites:
Pumpkin seeds
Prickley ash berries
Cayenne
Garlic
(In acute cases use any of the above and treat as with a cold)

COLITIS (Ulcerated Colon)

Up to 4 caps. slippery elm daily
Up to 6 caps. CS or CT daily
Up to 1 Tbsp. Psyllium powder or flake in glass of water or juice
before bedtime or
Up to 1 Tbsp. chia seed, ground

CUSHING'S DISEASE (ATCH Hormone)

Alfalfa — up to 20 tablets daily or
Chlorophyll — approx. 4 tbsp. in water or
Fresh alfalfa — approx. 3 tsp. daily
Vitamins and minerals:
Multiple vitamin
Calcium
Vitamin E
B complex
Vitamin C

CROUP

Laxative — empty stomach — enema
Lemon and honey (straight), one spoonful at a time, every 15 mins.
Cold wash cloth or ice pack around neck, with a dry towel on top
Keep neck cold until swelling goes down

DIABETES

Goldenseal — up to 20 caps. daily or
Juniper berries, chewed — up to 6-8 twice daily
Mild food diet
For parasites, formula or pumpkin seeds for small children
Vitamin B complex
Calcium
Vitamin E
Multiple vitamin

DIPTHERIA

Straight lemon & honey every half hour to clear throat
*Antispasmatic Tincture —
   Emetic:
   Cayenne, ginger, or bayberry
   Lobelia
   Equal parts in a tea
   Enema: (any of)
      Bayberry
      Catnip
      Chickweed
      Raspberry
      Strawberry
Hot baths — mustard & cayenne

DIABETIC WOUNDS

Powdered goldenseal

*Kloss, Back to Eden, p. 274

DYSPEPSIA (excessive acid, gas, lack of tone in digestive track) ·

Any one is helpful:
Bayberry
Lemon
Goldenseal
Sage
Yarrow
Ginger
Camomile
Spearmint
Blood root
Cayenne
Gentian root
Thyme
Related causes:
Cardiac — during heart attack
Fermentive — gas
Gastric — faulty stomach
Hepatic — liver

DIARRHEA

Psyllium powder or flake — approx. 1 tbsp. in glass of warm water or
Chia seed, ground — approx. 1 tbsp. in glass of warm water
Pain — approx. ½ to ¼ tsp. slippery elm

DRUGS (LSD, etc.)

Mild diet
High nutrition
Raw juice
High Vitamin B factor
Sunshine, fresh air, rest,
High Vitamin C — approx. 4,000-6,000 mg. daily
When glands have been damaged, see adrenal
When drug ring shows on the eyes, drugs are still in the body in the
area shown

ESTROGEN (Female hormone)

Black cohosh

ECZEMA

Chia — soak in warm water until thick, place on affected area —
stops pain — as pain returns, change poultice
Clean blood — see kidney herbs
Clean bowels

EARACHE

Ice bag on ear
Feet in hot mustard or cayenne water
Enema
Stop eating — only fruit & juice
Approx. 1,000 mg. Vit. C each hour
Laxative teas draw mucus from the ear:
        Horsetail ⎫
        Juniper   ⎬ for kidneys
        Alfalfa   ⎭

EMPHYSEMA

Lung herb — approx. 4 caps. daily
CS Formula — approx. 6 caps. daily
Mild food diet, raw juice
Approx. 2,000 mg. Vitamin C daily
Multiple vitamin

FATIGUE

Causes:
        Overeating
        Clogged system

Lack of oxygen
Lack of nutrition
Lack of exercise
Lack of proper elimination
Helpful aids:
Clean system
Correct breathing
Proper foods
Exercise
Proper attitude

FEVER

Enema
Same as for cold
Sponge baths with cool water when temp. gets too high (104 degrees)
Enema will usually bring fever right down

FEMALE FORMULA

To be taken orally for female problems:
Squaw vine — 1 part
Marshmallow — 1 part
Parsley — 1½ parts
Ginger — ½ part
Licorice — 1 part
Stillingia — 1 part
Lobelia — ½ part
Black Cohosh — 1 part

Vaginal suppository:
Squaw vine
Slippery elm
Yellow dock
Goldenseal

Use melted cocoa butter, add herbs, form into 2" suppository, put on waxed paper in refrigerator. Insert for 3 nights and douche (see Vaginal Discharge) each of 3 mornings.

Use for fibroid tumors — intermittent bleeding — use between periods of hemorrhage

FROST BITE

Cayenne — approx. ¼ tsp. every 2 hours

GANGRENE (Blood poisoning)
Afflicted area:
Marshmallow root tea packs or
Soaking in tea is faster — add small amount of lobelia for pain
Clean system
Fruit only
Vitamin C

GOUT (Excess uric acid — cause)
Tincture of lobelia with apple cider vinegar and honey
Vinegar bath
Laxative herbs
3 days of orange, grapefruit & lemon juice — after 3 days, treat as
    arthritis

GINGER helpful in
Boils
Bronchitis
Cholera
Colds
Colic
Congestion
Diarrhea
Gas
Flu
Gout
Headache
Hemorrhage
Lungs
Menstrual cramps
Nausea
Neuralgia
Paralysis of tongue
Rheumatism
Sore throat
Toothache

GALLSTONES
Laxative
No meals after noon
Bedtime:
    Up to ½ cup straight lemon
    Up to ½ cup cold pressed olive oil

Morning: (following day)
Enema — gallstones removed will show up in stool

GONORRHEA

Better nutrition
Mild foot diet
Clean blood
Burdock
Cleaver
Goldenseal
Hops
Parsley
Juniper berries
Squaw vine

HEART ATTACK

Hot cayenne tea — approx. 1 tsp. cayenne (attack can stop in about 2 min.)

HEMORRHAGE

Up to 1 tsp. cayenne in extra warm water will stop bleeding fast
For external bleeding put cayenne on wound

HAIR RINSE

Nettle — helpful in restoring color
Camomile
Sage

HIGH BLOOD PRESSURE

Lecithin — up to 3 tsp. daily, powder
Cayenne — up to 1 tsp. in water daily
Cactus liquid — up to 10 drops daily

HODGKINS DISEASE

High potassium diet
Clean blood
High Vitamin C
Mild food diet
Potassium gluconate
Iodine (liquid) or
Kelp (tablet) or
Dulse (tablet)

HEMORRHOIDS

Suppository:
>   Glycerine or cocoa butter
>   Goldenseal — 2 parts
>   Bayberry — 2 parts
>   Chickweed — 2 parts
>   Witch hazel bark — ¼ part
>   Catnip — ¼ part
>   Form and place in refrigerator to harden

Fruit diet for a few days, then mild food
High potassium foods
High Vitamin C
Slippery elm — approx. 3-4 caps. daily
No cheese

HAYFEVER

Stop eating, except fruit
Clean blood
Up to 1,000 mg. Vit. C. each hour
Comfrey
Alfalfa mint
Red clover
Horsetail
Violet
Eyewash: (use eye cup)
>   Eyebright
>   Goldenseal
>   Bayberry
>   also drops in nose

HIVES

Teas:
>   Chickweed
>   Comfrey
>   Burdock Root
>   Nettle
>   Camomile
>   Hops
>   Black Cohosh
>   Peppermint
>   Alfalfa

Approx. 1,000 mg. Vit. C each hour

Laxative

Enema

Citrus juice (if not the cause)

HYPERGLYCEMIA (Low Blood Sugar, Addison's Disease)

Mild food only

Clean bowel

Where ulcers have formed in bowel, slippery elm

For acid burning — Vit. B complex & calcium are helpful

Sleep & rest, stay away from stress situations, overcome worry & fear

Licorice, or Mexican wild yam

Goldenseal — ½ as much as licorice

High mineral foods:

    Potassium

    Sodium

    Calcium

    Magnesium

High B Complex, plus Paba, B6, B3

INSOMNIA

Relaxant Herbs:

Hops or

Valerian tea

Best tranquilizer I know of:

    Vitamin B. Complex

    Calcium lactate

INFLAMMATION

Cayenne — up to 1 tsp. each hour until pain is gone

Alfalfa mint tea — up to 1 cup each hour

In female organs — female formula suppositories or chlorophyll
    douche

Bowel — CT Formula

Lungs — lung herb

Throat — glycerine & iodine

Eyes — eye wash or goldenseal

High Vitamin C

JAUNDICE

Any acute disease should be treated as with a cold

Lemon is one of the best cleansers of the liver there is, along with
    Vit. C and mild food

KIDNEY INFECTION

Enema
Vitamin C
Goldenseal
Juniper oil
Potassium gluconate will take off fluid — approx. 9 600 mg. tablets
Kidney herbs:
  Cornsilk
  Goldenseal
  Juniper berries
  Dandelion
  Alfalfa
  Sassafras

KIDNEY STONE

STOP all eating
Juice of one lemon in small amount of water every time pain comes on, continue until stones are dissolved
Goldenseal — approx. 3-4 caps. daily, if no low blood sugar.
Hot enema when pain is down
Lobelia or other relaxant tea
Usually not necessary to take lemon juice longer than 12-14 hours.

Kidney stones will dissolve with lemon, as water on rock salt, melting away the sharp edges. These sharp edges cut like glass on their way through, causing swelling and intense pain. With a kidney stone the pain can be as severe as a difficult delivery of a baby. A man who has passed a kidney stone knows what a difficult birth can be like. The taking of lemon juice is such an easy thing and works so well, it is hard for me to understand why medical science has not discovered so simple a remedy.

LAXATIVE HERBS

Mandrake or
Cascara Sagrada or
Senna

LUNG HERB

Mullein — 1 part
Comfrey — 1 part
Marshmallow — 1 part
Slippery elm — 1 part
Lobelia — ½ part

MULTIPLE SCLEROSIS

Is nutritional and usually caused by a bruise
Formula — herbal parasite — approx. 4 (00 size) caps. daily
Herb to cleanse — CT or CS, approx. 6 daily
Raw vegetable juice
Raw food (nothing cooked)
Vitamin therapy:
> Vitamin E
> Vitamin B Complex
> Calcium
> Vitamin C
> Magnesium
> Folic Acid
> Vitamin B3, Niacin
> Multiple vitamin and mineral

MUSTARD PLASTER

3 tbsp. flour
2 tbsp. lard
1 tbsp. mustard, dry
1 tbsp. each:
> Spirits of turpentine
> Glycerine
Spread on a cloth as large as chest

MALARIA

To kill parasite, black walnut
Grapefruit rinds boiled is natural quinine
Cachono bark

MENSTRUAL CRAMPS

Ginger tea
Black cohosh — approx. ½ tsp.
Calcium
Heating pad or hot bath
For menstrual obstruction:
> Peppermint — 1 part
> Wood betony — 1 part
> (Approx. a wine glassful every 3 hours)

NERVOUSNESS

Hops tea

Catnip tea
Camomile tea
Lobelia — combine with others, small amount only
Nerve Formula

NERVE FORMULA

Lady slipper
Valarian
Mistletoe
Hops
Black cohosh
Wood Betony
Lobelia
Scullcap
Goldenseal

NURSING

Lots of fruit for mother
When baby has a cold, mother take up to 1,000 mg. Vit. C. hourly,
  stay on fruit, take laxative
Caked breast:
  Hot & cold packs
  Be sure to empty breast each time

NOSEBLEED

Cayenne — approx. ½ tsp. in water

NAUSEA

Peppermint tea
Alfalfa mint tea
Where nervousness is the cause:
  Catnip
  Hops
  Red clover
In pregnancy:
  Goldenseal
  Calcium
  Vitamin B6

PARASITES (Formula for)

Culver's root — 1 part
Mandrake — 1 part

Violet leaves — 1 part
Powdered pumpkin seed — 2 parts
Poke root — ⅛ part
Cascara sagrada — ⅛ part
Witch hazel bark — ⅛ part
Mullein — ⅛ part
Comfrey — ⅛ part
Slippery elm powder — ⅛ part

PLEURISY

Lung Herb — up to 4 caps. daily
Mild food diet, or fruit if acute
Vitamin C — up to 6,000 mg. daily

PINEAL GLAND FORMULA

Equal parts:
  Chickweed
  Pink root
  Comfrey
Cyani flowers — ¾ part
Approx. 1 (00 size) caps. morning, noon and night
Approx. 3 caps. daily

PARASITES (Amoebic dysentery)

Herbal parasite formula — approx. 4 caps. daily
Pumpkin seeds
Heal all — approx. 2 caps. daily
Nettle — approx. 2 caps. daily

POISON OAK OR IVY

Up to 2,000 mg. Vit. C each hour
Goldenseal ointment
Fruit and juice until rash is gone

PYORRHEA

Goldenseal & myrrh as a mouthwash

PROSTATE GLAND

Clean bowel
Pumpkin seeds or herbal parasite formula to kill parasites
Buchu tea
Hot bath

PUNCTURE WOUND
Bleed
Soak in hot water
Treat as with cold
Herb poultice — comfrey, etc.

PARKINSON'S DISEASE (Palsy)
Mild food diet
Lots of raw juice
Vitamin B1, daily
Multiple vitamin, daily
B complex, daily
Calcium, daily
Vitamin B12, daily

PHLEBITIS
Stop eating — fruit & juice only
Vitamin C — approx. 1,000 mg. each hour for 2 days
Hot and cold packs
Stay on fruit until inflammation is clear
Mild food diet until after pregnancy and while nursing
Vitamin C & Vitamin E are important for keeping
    the tone of the veins

PREGNANCY
Spikenard:
    Approx. 1 cap. daily the month before delivery
    Approx. 2 caps. daily 2 weeks before delivery
    Approx. 3 caps. daily the last week
Blue cohosh at hospital
2 months on desert tea — approx. 2-3 cups daily
Strawberry & raspberry tea — approx. 2-3 cups
    daily the entire 9 months

STROKE (Apoplexy)
Cayenne — approx. ½ tsp. and
Mustard — approx. ½ tsp. place in hot bath until
    patient sweats profusely
Cayenne — approx. 1 tsp. in warm water to drink
Parsley & lecithin help to clean arteries
Mild food diet

STIMULANTS
Cayenne
Ginger
Snake root
Peppermint
Cloves
Horseradish
Black Pepper
Prickly ash

SYPHILIS
(is a nutritional disease and not entirely a disease of sin)
Yellow dock
Bayberry
Barberry
Blue violet
Red clover
Prickly ash berries
Bugleweed
Blood root
Bitter root
Clean blood
Vit. C — approx. 4,000 mg. daily
Mild food diet
Raw juice
High vitamin & mineral diet & supplements

SORE THROAT
Glycerine & iodine — swab throat every hour
Straight lemon & honey
Throat or tongue paralysis;
 Cayenne — approx. 1 tsp.
 Apple cider vinegar — approx. 2 tbsp.
 Sage tea — approx. ½ pint
 Sea salt — approx. 2 tbsp.
 Honey — approx. 2 tbsp.
 (Gargle with above 4-12 times daily)

TB
(Is a disease of poor nutrition and lung deterioration)
Clean blood
Vitamin C — approx. 4,000 mg. daily

Sunshine, fresh air, rest, exercise
Raw juice therapy
Lung herbs
High vitamin & mineral supplements

THYROID (Hormone)

Liquid iodine — approx. 3 drops
Myxedemia — up to 40-50
Kelp — dulce — approx. 4-6 tablets

TONSILITIS

Paint every hour with glycerine & iodine
Mix in clear bottle glycerine & add iodine until
    color is deep amber
Mild food diet except when acute —
    then fruits only and treat as with a cold

ULCER OF STOMACH

Mild food diet
Vitamin C — approx. 2,000 mg.
Up to 2 Okra tablets or 3 caps.
    powdered 20 mins. before meals
Up to 2 caps. slippery elm 20 mins. before meals

ULCER (Running Sore)

CS — approx. 6 caps. daily
Clean blood
Tonic herbs
Goldenseal on open wound
Bayberry poultice
Mullein poultice
Comfrey, fresh

VAGINAL DISCHARGE

When acute, treat as with a cold
Clean blood
Mild food diet
Douche; (any one)
    Bayberry — approx. ½ tsp. in water bag
    Chlorophyll — approx. 1½ tsp. in water bag
    Goldenseal — approx. ½ tsp. in water bag
Herb pack for vaginal use:

Melt cocoa butter
Squaw vine
Chickweed
Yellow dock
Goldenseal
Mullein
Marshmallow
Black cohosh
(form into suppositories, place on waxed paper
    in refrigerator to cool)

VIRUS DISEASES (Measles, Mumps, Chickenpox, Smallpox,
    Pneumonia, Polio, Typhoid)
Stop eating
Fruit and fruit juice only
Herb laxative, enema
Vitamin C — approx. 1,000-2,000 an hour
Hot saffron tea or boiled grapefruit rind & fruit
    (strain and drink hot) to help break out
    where fever is high
Wild carrot
Treat as with cold

FEVER

Fever is nature's way of bringing impurities to the surface and is also nature's way of warning that all systems are clogged, and help is needed immediately. A fever has been described as a car running with its brakes on. Fever only occurs when other channels of elimination are not removing waste material fast enough, or when they are stopped. Again, do as with the common cold — help nature. Usually an enema will bring the fever right down. Vitamin C, fruit, and many herbs will assist in such cases. Goldenseal is antibiotic and helps to kill germs. It is good to keep the body covered and warm. Cayenne is exceptionally good when irregularity of the heart exists or when it beats too fast. The heart will always beat faster during a disease crisis or when taking high doses of Vitamin C.

ASTHMA

Most asthmatics have the same physical appearance; a deep cup area just below the ribs; too much mucus in the lung area — caused sometimes from a short diaphragm; and an inability to eat larger quantities of food, especially gas-forming foods. Personality characteristics are the inability to cope with stress, causing the stomach to shut off at the duodenum, refusing to empty, with the resulting increase of gas and putrefaction, causing a toxic condition of the entire chest cavity. Sometimes, adrenal insufficiency can cause the inability to cope with the stress when they are not secreting enough cortin or related hormones.

BOILS (rash, pimples, etc.)

These are caused from too much mucus in the blood, eliminating through the skin when the bowel and kidneys are not performing well. The skin is often affected when there is adrenal insufficiency. Asthmatics tend often to skin rash, due to inability to cope with stress. However, without the mucus in the lung, there would not be an asthma attack.

MEASLES

Measles can be avoided, like all other contagious disease, if the body is clean and well-nourished (see section on common cold, use same treatment). There are many herbs which will help in case of measles, either to bring the breaking-out into full bloom, or to help after breaking-out has occured. Saffron tea taken quite warm (never boil) will cause a break-out if measles are suspected and fever persists after an enema. Also the juice of a boiled grapefruit rind or alfalfa mint tea helps. A soda bath helps to alkalize the skin. To soothe the itching child, a warm catnip enema is helpful. You can give him a tea using approximately 1 tsp. pleurisy root and ¼ tsp. (approx.) ginger; steep this in boiled water. (Never boil herbs - steep only.) Camomile tea, vervaine, yarrow, and lady slipper may also be used.

COMMON COLD

The common cold is nature's way to save life. If you eat wrong and say, "I never have a cold," there is usually a chronic toxic condition in the head area. A cold is nature cleaning your house so you can continue life. When your body builds toxic waste to a dangerous point — if you have a good vitality — your body will force a disease crisis, anything from a cold to the flu, all virus diseases, or contagious diseases. You will always feel better after the crisis than before. Nature at this time does not always clean down to immaculate cleanliness. Nature only cleans until nutrition is again required to maintain your body strength, then soon may force another crisis and clean some more. This is why you may keep having one cold after another or have pneumonia two of three times. Of course the thing we usually do as soon as our house has been swept a little is to fill it again with unnatural toxic foods. It is like sweeping trash out one door as fast as you sweep it in the other. You can never get ahead of it.

What about the germ theory? Germs do not live and multiply where they have no food. Bacteria, parasites, etc. live on the refuse of the body. If you keep your body clean and well-nourished — this means mentally and spiritually as well as physically — you have no need to fear the microbe.

When a cold occurs you have earned it, so relax and enjoy this process as nature strives to save your life. You can help her by using only fruits and herbs and eliminating all mucus-forming foods.

Fruits are the highest in ascorbic acid and glucose sugar. The combination of the two (and I do not know how it works) seems to dissolve mucus, drawing from the lymph of the entire body and sending it on through the kidneys, as well as acting as a laxative to the sludge in the bowel.

You can also assist nature by an herbal laxative and an enema to make way for the rest of the toxic debris which will follow. This method will shorten the time nature requires to get the job done. High doses of Vitamin C (straight ascorbic acid in acute sickness — 1,000 to 2,000 mgs. an hour) accelerates the process, dissolving the mucus rapidly and sending it on through the kidneys and bowels. I have seen time and time again that an herbal laxative, Vitamin C, and a fruit diet will clean the body (a cold) in a day or two, where it would ordinarily require two to three weeks.

Measles, mumps, chicken pox., etc., can be avoided entirely if this process is used immediately upon exposure. Here again, clean the blood and the body, and the contagion cannot take hold.

Without this above help, often so much mucus floods the kidneys as to cause a break in the kidney filter, causing Bright's Disease (Nephritis). Other diseases draining continual infections weaken the kidneys, such as infected teeth, tonsils, and other chronic infections. Constant chronic infections are the breeding grounds for germ growths and cause much of the eventually forced elimination and much of the fatigue people experience from day to day. This is why you will feel so much better after a heavy elimination (house cleaning — cold) or after having gone on a cleansing diet.

There is, however, a great difference between the disease crisis and the healing crisis, as has been pointed out. As soon as the person reaches a certain degree of vitality by continual correct diet, they will sometimes experience a healing crisis. The healing crisis differs in that you will be sick only long enough to remove the remainder of the debris, and then the body will often be clean (spotless). When vitality, or ability to throw off waste, is less, nature will only clean a little at a time; and you may have small, periodic healing crises. When an extensive healing crisis occurs, it always occurs when the person has been on a corrective cleansing diet for an extended period and is to a point of feeling marvelous, or the best they have felt in years. Nature never causes a healing crisis until the person has reached the point of vitality where he can stand the shock.

In a disease crisis it is rare that Vitamin C, (straight ascorbic acid), needs to be taken longer than four or five days in high doses. If taken longer, as in cases of polio, etc., calcium and Vitamin B complex should be added, as well as a multiple vitamin, because straight ascorbic acid leeches the vitamins, etc., especially calcium and Vitamin B. Nature will usually bring the elimination to a halt when more nutrition is needed, except in cases of terminal leukemia, where the body is literally strangling in mucus (white cells) and cannot stop the elimination. In an attempt to up the red count, medical science adds blood, often with so much mucus filling the bloodstream that the added blood will run out the mouth and/or nose. So far I do not know of anyone who has been cured in this way, but they continue to make the same mistakes, adding a protein and mucus diet to an already overly-encumbered body, then adding the painful transfusions of other people's blood. Here again, it costs a lot to die of leukemia — about 100 transfusions at $100 each. It turns out to be big business yet leukemia is probably one of the easiest terminal diseases to overcome, as the waste, especially in children, is already on the move in the blood. Chronic disease is a little harder to dig out. I mention leukemia here because it is almost in the class of an acute disease; it has been discussed with colds and can be helped in the same way. The difference is that in a cold, nature will usually stop the elimination (except in pneumonia) before death occurs, giving the body a chance to build up again before she again digs deeper. Leukemia, like a bad case of pneumonia, where the body is so overly encumbered with waste (like running downhill) cannot stop until the person is dead. When we learn to assist nature in her determined course rather than to put more fuel on the fire, leukemia need no longer be a terminal disease. It is necessary to give the same treatment as with a cold for four days at a time, then back to the CS herbs and mild food, using a multiple vitamin and mineral, taking over the eliminating and building process nature is unable at this point to do herself.

117

Some of the other diseases considered terminal, such as Bright's Disease and Multiple Sclerosis, have been found by people using nature's methods not to be terminal. They have used mild food, raw only, and high doses of vitamins and minerals, along with herbs. These are diseases nutritionally caused or brought on by damage of some sort, where nutrition has not been sufficient to heal. In bringing the body back up to a highly nourished state, the disease has often been overcome.

Tuberculosis is in this class, as well as the diseases of sin (venereal). India has the highest death rate by tuberculosis, as many live in a famine and starving situation all of their lives. The body merely deteriorates in certain areas on its way to death's consummation. It has been seen how a starving person will break out in running sores that will not heal. Nature starts an elimination, as has been said, when in a famine or fasting condition. In cases where fasting is continued too long, with only occasional relief from hunger, and usually with poor food, the body continues to throw off the waste, much like leukemia (running downhill unable to stop).

Where venereal disease is becoming a threat to our young people, it is thought the cause is the loosening of morals; however, this is not entirely the case. When young people become involved in and preoccupied with drugs and sex, as has been the case, they are either away from the protection of mother's table or the drugs and the sex become their sole interest, causing the body to deteriorate from lack of proper nourishment. When we couple the lack of enough good food with the drugs and the fasting or famine condition many of the youngsters have become subject to by their own choice or from not having their parents to supply their needs, like tuberculosis the diseases of sin spread rapidly among young, deteriorating bodies. What a waste.

If necessary nutrients are added, building the strength; adding also nature's three healing angels (as the Apocryphal book, *The Essene Gospel* puts it: sun, water, and air) the body will usually heal itself of these diseases considered to be terminal.

There has not been enough emphasis in this book placed on the healing powers of air, sun, and water. Many of us find too little time to breathe fresh air, to be out in the sun. We have been brainwashed with the idea that too much sun causes cancer. Let me say this in defense of the wondrous healing powers of the sun: if you develop cancer from being out in the sun, it was because nature's sun was only the instrument to bring to the surface cancer already in the body. Any burning of the skin, of course, can do damage. It is best to enjoy water with the sun bath, cooling and moisturizing the skin; then a tan can be a beautiful and healthy experience.

The water we drink is another long story that goes without telling. Find some pure, undefiled water if health is what you desire.

John Elliotson said,

"True philosophers compelled by the love of truth and wisdom, never fancy themselves so wise and full of sense as not to yield to truth from any source and at all times; nor are they so narrow minded as to believe any art or science has been handed down in such a state of perfection to us by our predecessors that nothing remains for future industry."

CHAPTER FIVE

MORE ANTIDOTES — THE VITAMINS

What is going to happen when and if the F.D.A. closes all health food stores? They seem to be moving in this direction. If you have had a definite testimony and help from natural vitamins, what will you do? A health food store saleslady, when asked recently on a TV show (when it was announced that vitamins A and D would be removed from the market), "What will people do?" answered, "Get it on the black market." Has Satan set another snare for the fine people who have learned the value of truth? Will the vitamin remain in the hands of the people of integrity who have made the vitamin in a natural way, when it must be sold only on the black market? Will the vitamin/mineral supplements remain natural if these people of integrity have to turn criminal to sell their products? Will they turn criminal, or will the criminal move in on a good operation to make money on the disappointed public who feel they must have vitamins to live and be well?

The better answer would be to obey the law and find another way to get vitamins from food and herbs. In order to get full vitamin value from your food, you must first clean the blood, clear the toxic waste from your body, then learn the foods rich in the vitamins you need. Second, you must discover by certain symptoms which vitamins or minerals you may be lacking and add foods or herbs rich in these things. Then you must make sure that the foods contain the vitamin and mineral value. There has been a lot written against poisons and sprays, chemical fertilizers, etc. If you are to receive the highest vitamin and mineral value from your food, it stands to reason that the food itself must have also been fed in the best way.

Many years ago my uncle, who was a "horticulturist," ran his own private test when the new chemical fertilizers first came on the market. Taking two tomato plants and planting them side by side with one stake between them on which they could both climb, having prepared the soil on the one side with chemical fertilizer and the other with organic matter compost, he began his vigil to see just what would happen. The plants began to grow, climbing the stake together, intertwining with one another. As they grew larger, he began to observe the difference in vigor, beauty, and health of the organically composted plant. He noticed aphids beginning to come onto the plant feeding on the chemical ground. Strange how it didn't affect the stronger organic plant. What could he do to save the sick plant? The only thing he could have done, and this is the answer people find today: spray it with poison to kill the bugs. Does this tell you anything?

Years ago when most of my children were young, we were having a hard time keeping them well on the poor, undernourished, chemically-raised food we bought on the market, so we decided we should find a small piece of ground and go to organic gardening. Our place had almost every kind of fruit. We dried prunes, apricots, and corn on the garage roof and had our own bees and beautiful spring water gravity flow to the house and fields. We had some very interesting experiences. The first year, the ground being prepared with compost, we had some worms in the corn; but the second year, not one. We raised beautiful, healthily-nourished food, and our children bloomed into gorgeous health.

After four years of never needing or taking a vitamin, we moved back to the city. What a change took place in all of us; and we have been struggling ever since to keep our heads above water, so to speak.

Living in a poisoned world is not easy at best. Even knowing what I do about how to supplement our diets with natural vitamins, our health has never been as it was when we received our vitamins from nature's own table. Still, I compare my family's health with that of the people around us, and I am thankful for the knowledge I have of vitamin/mineral values. Knowing what I do, I should be smart enough to leave this "rat race" and go back to the land. Maybe we should all be smart enough. Perhaps the world situation will force us to do the right thing.

There has been a great deal written about vitamins and minerals. It is not my intention to convince you of their necessity in your body, but rather to show you where you can get them from your food, as well as in natural pill form. It is my hope that I have convinced you sufficiently about natural vitamins from organic food sources — the only way, if results are what you are seeking.

When or if you begin to use vitamin therapy, do not do as many have done, who have been discouraged with vitamins because they take only one thing at a time. Often after reading an article in a health magazine, we tend to think, "Ah ha, that sounds just like what I need." Off we go to the store to buy a single vitamin. To gain any real results from vitamins, you must take a balanced multiple vitamin first, and then add the restorative doses of any one vitamin or mineral your body may need over and above the multiple. When you have added the restorative dose for awhile and the symptom for which you were taking it returns to normal, it is no longer necessary to continue to take high restorative doses. A daily multiple dose is all that is necessary, with, of course, the exception being during an acute illness when all food and vitamins should be discontinued to a fasting or semi-fasting state (see section on colds).

When the body is clean and fed from nature's table, vitamins and minerals are absorbed like a sponge. When the body is sickly and full of waste, more vitamins are needed to bring the body into a better balance so nature can throw off the waste, as has been shown with leukemia. In other words, build sufficient vitality so the body will move the waste. Then as you begin a heavy periodic acute elimination, vitamin supplements should be stopped. In this way you restore and clean, making a more comfortable process to regain health. It is not correct to fast a weak person clear down to clean, or dead. Sometimes it can be both. It is better to gain in strength as you go along, and your body will eliminate when it feels strong enough to stand the shock (note disease crisis).

I knew of a woman who had multiple sclerosis who had not walked for eleven years. After cleansing her body, killing the parasites and building enough vitality, she began a healing crisis that lasted for about three days. After it was over, she walked for the first time in eleven years. A healing crisis is a marvel to watch.

The foods listed below are high in the vitamins or minerals shown. Where ** or *** appears, there is an abundance.

A
(small amounts in all foods)
watermelon
raw carrot juice
yellow & green foods

Herbs

alfalfa
dandelion
lamsquarter
okra pods
paprika
parsley
cayenne
grape leaves
red raspberry
violet

B

almonds
brazil nuts
coconut
haddock
poultry
**veal
ice cream
honey
molasses
yeast
alfalfa
artichokes
**asparagus
beans
soy beans
**beets
broccoli
**Brussels sprouts
**carrots
**cauliflower
cabbage
celery
cucumbers
lentils
leeks
**lettuce
molasses
mushrooms
okra
parsley

peanuts
parsnips
peas
peppers
potatoes
**rutabagas
sauerkraut
tomatoes
turnips
**barley
wheat
corn
rye
apples
avocados
**bananas
cantaloupe
dates
**figs
oranges
peaches
raisins
**strawberries
**watermelon
yogurt
honey
milk

B1 (Thiamine)

bladderwrack
dulse
kelp
fenugreek
dandelion
grape leaves
red raspberry
okra
wheat germ

B^2 (Riboflavin)

bladderwrack
dulse
fenugreek

kelp
saffron
wild rose hip

B^{12} (Cobalt)

alfalfa
bladderwrack
kelp
dulse

B^3 (Niacin)

same as other &
blueberry

B^{17} (Nitrilosides)

fruit seeds
apricot seeds
bamboo shoots
aquatic grass
flax seed
lima beans
burma beans
scarlet runners
lentils
rangoon beans

B Complex herbs

valerian
hops
catnip
red clover

C

***raw goat milk
beets
**brussel sprouts
carrots
**cauliflower
eggplant
**endive
lentils
leeks

**peppers
  rhubarb
  turnips
  rutabagas
  sweet potatoes
**sauerkraut
**strawberries
**tomatoes
**turnips
***watercress
  bananas
  cherries
**oranges
  apricots
  peaches
  watermelon

C-herbs

**burdock seed
**coltsfoot
***elderberries
  marigold

  oregano
  paprika
  parsley
***rosehips
***watercress
  lobelia
  dandelion
  grape leaves
  hawthorn berries
  plantain
  red raspberry leaves
  violet

(Vitamin C destroyed in
cooking, by light, by too
much copper, by too much
iron, and baking soda)

D

sunshine
sunlamp
cream
milk
egg yolk
cod liver oil
alfalfa
***lettuce

herbs
annato seed
wheatgerm
***watercress

E

most vegetables
***goat milk
green leafy vegetables
small amounts in all things
wheatgerm and oil
soy oil
all oils
nut oil
seeds
dried beans
whole grain
red raspberry leaves
rosehip

G

**broccoli
cabbage
peas

herbs
alfalfa
avena satira
dandelion
dulse
kelp
linseed
sesame seed

watercress
hydrocotyle asiatica
gotu kola
grape leaves
red raspberry leaves

K

alfalfa
chestnuts
shepherds purse
green leafy vegetables
cabbage
cauliflower
plantain

P (Rutin)

buckwheat
paprika
gernan
rue

H (Biotin)

yeast
unpolished rice
soy flour
soy beans
(trace vitamin)

CALCIUM

beef
lamb
liver
***pancreas
***poultry
veal
buttermilk
cheese
***cottage cheese
goat cheese
**swiss cheese
cream
eggs
**artichokes
walnuts

asparagus
**lima beans
**beets (leaves & root)
**broccoli
**brussel sprouts
**carrots
cauliflower
**celery
endive
**okra
parsley
parsnips
peas
potatoes
rhubarb
**rutabagas
***sauerkraut
**squash
tomatoes
turnips (tops & root)
watercress
rye bread
**whole wheat bread
corn
***hominy
rice
rye
wheat
apples
avocados
bananas
blueberries
dates
**figs
olives
oranges
**peaches
peas
raisins
raspberries
**coconut
***filberts
hickory nuts
peanuts

herbs (Calcium)

arrow root
carragreen
chamomile
chives
cleaver
coltsfoot
dandelion
flax seed
horsetail
meadow sweet
mistletoe
nettle
sorrel
okra pods
plantain
shepherds purse
red raspberry leaves

CHLORINE

alfalfa
raw goat milk
honey
eggs
small amounts in most foods,
especially vegetables
present in salt

PHOSPHORUS

yeast
alfalfa
**artichokes
**kale
lentils
leeks
lettuce
mushrooms
mustard greens
onions
pumpkin
turnips
oatmeal
rice
**rye

wheat
apricots
bananas
cherries
cranberries
**dates
pineapple
prunes
small amount in most foods

Herbs (Phosphorus)
calamus
caraway seeds
sesame seeds
okra
sorrel
watercress
chickweed
marigold
garlic
licorice
meadow sweet flower
alfalfa
red raspberry leaves

MAGNESIUM
alfalfa
lentils
**leeks
***lettuce leaf
mushrooms
mustard greens
onions
**parsnips
peas
potatoes
spinach
sauerkraut
***tomatoes
turnips
***watercress
barley
rye

wheat
***corn
small amount in most foods

Herbs

bladderwrack
black willow bark
carrot leaves
dulse
dandelion
kale
kelp
meadow sweet
parsley
skunk cabbage
walnut leaves
wintergreen
mistletoe
mullein
okra

IRON

132

molasses
pumpkin
small amount in all foods

Herbs
burdock
devils bit
meadow sweet
mullein
parsley
red raspberry leaves
rest harrow
silverweed
stinging nettle
strawberry leaves
watercress
yellow dock
dandelion

SULPHUR

**poultry
***veal
butter
buttermilk
cheese
***raw goat milk
molasses
**asparagus
soy beans
lima beans
beets
broccoli
**carrots
***cauliflower
celery
chard
eggplant
***endive
lentils
***lettuce
mushrooms
mustard greens
cooked onions
parsley
**parsnips
peas
peppers
**potatoes
sweet potatoes
***peaches
peas
raisins
pumpkin
radishes
rhubarb
rutabagas
sauerkraut
tomatoes
turnips (tops & roots)
watercress
barley
**whole wheat

```
  **corn
***rice
    wheat germ
    apricots
***bananas
    blueberries
    blackberries
    cantaloupe
    cherries
    cranberries
  **dates
***figs
    gooseberries
    grapefruit
    grapes
    lemons
    limes
***olives
***oranges
    raspberries
***watermelon
    coconut
    filberts
  **hickory nuts
  **peanuts
    pecans
    walnuts
```

134

Herbs
calamus
carragreen
coltsfoot
eyebright
fennel
garlic
mullein
okra
stinging nettle
watercress
waywart
shepherds purse
plantain leaves
silverweed
**alfalfa

POTASSIUM

milk
molasses
broccoli
cabbage,(cooked)
carrots
cauliflower
**celery
chard
**cucumbers
eggplant
endive
**kale
lentils
leeks
***lettuce
mushroom
mustard greens
onions
**cooked onions
parsley
parsnips
peas
potatoes
**sweet potatoes
**pumpkin
**radishes
**rutabagas
sauerkraut
spinach
**squash
**tomatoes
turnips,(tops & roots)
**watercress
barley
rye
corn
**oatmeal
**rice
apples
**apricots
avocados
**blueberries

**blackberries
**cherries
**cranberries
**dates
***figs
   gooseberries
   limes
**peaches, canned
   peas
   pineapple
**prunes, fresh or dried
   strawberries
**watermelon
   brazil nuts
   chestnuts
**hickory nuts
**peanuts
   walnuts
   haddock
   herring
**salmon
***beef

   lamb
   buttermilk
   cheese
   cream
**eggs
   milk

Herbs
birch bark
calamus
carragreen
carrot leaves
chamomile flowers
coltsfoot
comfrey
dandelion
eye bright
fennel
mistletoe
mullein
nettle
oak bark

parsley
peppermint
plantain
primrose
sanicle
watercress
yarrow
alfalfa

FLUORINE

***raw goat milk
garlic
watercress
only traces in other foods

IODINE

raw goat milk
broccoli
carrots
***peppers
rutabagas
 **turnips, root
***kelp
dulse (deep sea lettuce)

Herbs
bladderwrack
iceland moss
Irish moss

MANGANESE

beans
beet root
kale
lettuce
peas, dried
 **turnip (tops & root)
***barley
***corn
bananas
raspberries
 **almonds
***brazil nuts
coconut
filberts
walnuts
butter
 **swiss cheese

SODIUM

blueberries
cherries
cranberries
dates
gooseberries
**grapes
lemons
limes
**olives
**pears
pineapple
prunes, fresh or dried
strawberries
watermelon
**brazil nuts
chestnuts
coconut
**peanuts
**walnuts
**herring
**Limberger cheese
swiss cheese
***raw goat milk
***molasses
***alfalfa
asparagus
beans
carrots
cauliflower
chard
endive
**kale
***leeks
lettuce
okra
parsley
peas
potatoes
rhubarb
**rutabagas
**sauerkraut
**squash

138

tomatoes
**turnips
watercress
**barley
corn
rice
wheat
apples
avocado
bananas
***eggs
egg yolk

Herbs

black willow
carragreen
chives
cleaver
fennel
meadow sweet
mistletoe
alfalfa
dandelion

139

SILICON

raw goat milk
yeast
artichokes
asparagus
lima beans
***cauliflower
celery
chard
cucumbers
***endive
lentils
lettuce
mushroom
mustard greens
parsley
potatoes
pumpkin
rhubarb
tomatoes

turnips, tops & root
**barley
***rye
***whole wheat
***corn
rice
apricots
avocados
blueberries
**olives
**oranges
raspberries
strawberries
***almonds
brazil nuts
**coconut
liver
Limberger cheese

Herbs

alfalfa
horsetail

When there is a lack of certain vitamins in the diet, it has been found by much research, both private and governmental, that certain symptoms can be alleviated, or brought back to normal, by restorative doses. This has also been the case where mineral values are concerned. It has been found that both minerals and vitamins work together, and certain vitamin complexes work in conjunction with one another to bring about a change. It has been found that a person can take a daily multiple vitamin and mineral supplement and feel healthy and normal in all respects but one or two; and when the correct vitamin or mineral is added, over and above the multiple in restorative doses, the problem is solved. As has been stated, a multiple taken first gives a balance, then a restorative dose for any lack. You will observe sometimes as you read the following pages, the same symptoms involving each of several vitamins or minerals. Where this is the case, it would be necessary to take each one of these in restorative doses until the problem is alleviated, then back to only a daily minimum vitamin and mineral intake. It has been found that natural vitamins, when taken in large doses, are not any more toxic than food. Too much food can, however, be toxic, as I have shown. It is my opinion that when vitamins and mineral supplements are added in high doses to an already toxic body, they can add to the toxicity; or sometimes they act as a stimulant to move waste. To really gain the benefit, they should be taken after a three months' diet of herbs and mild food has cleansed the body sufficiently so they can be utilized. During an acute illness, as the body changes to an eliminative organ, the taking of vitamin supplements only adds to the confusion, with the exception of Vitamin C. Minerals stand in a different class than the feeding process of vitamins. Certain minerals act as a cleanser, as with herbs, and assist in cleansing and restoring somehow as they go along. I do not know how or why; I only know it is true.

It has and will always be my opinion that the best way to maintain a balance is by living on organically-grown healthy foods. Where we cannot acquire these, of course the antidote of food supplements are next best; but these must also be made from natural foods in order to be used by the body.

Listed will be only approximately restorative doses, according to the research that has been done. It is always my opinion that when you add a vitamin or a medicine to your diet, you should learn as much as you can about your problem and let the spirit direct you to the amounts. This is a far better gauge than any educated guess your doctor could make. You may learn to become aware of just what is happening in your own being. You may look at this and say, "What kind of a stupid statement is that?" When you learn to fast and clean your body and live by the spirit, you will understand what I am telling you. We have lived too long letting someone else decide our physical fate. It is time we learned who we are and what we are all about.

Beginning with Vitamin A, dosage has been too high in most supplements because it was cheap. The large amount made the package look impressive I suppose. Added to an already toxic diet, an over-toxic condition resulted. This has been the cause of Vitamin A being taken off the market. This of course is unreasonable, the way it would be to take all soap off the market because someone may be allergic to it. A change could have been made in the allowable amounts per package. Another reason for the toxic result is, of course, use of a synthetic vitamin.

VITAMIN A NECESSARY FOR

skin
hair
nails
eyes
lungs

arteries
combats infection
increases vitality
growth & immunity
assists in uptake & use of iodine
bones
teeth

SYMPTOMS OF THE LACK OF VITAMIN A

night blindness
impaired vision
difficulty to adapt to darkness
glued eyelids
skin troubles (acne, boils, impetigo)
dandruff
brittle nails & hari
loos of hearing
loss of taste
stone formations
psoriasis
warts
wrinkles
gallstones
liver problems

Vitamin B Complex includes thiamine, riboflavin, niacin, Vitamin B6, pantothenic acid, biotin, Vitamin B12, folic acid, choline, and inositol.

VITAMIN B COMPLEX NECESSARY FOR

gastro-intestinal function
nervous system
glandular system
general growth
blood
essential in digestion
lactation
healing
hair

SYMPTOMS OF LACK OF VITAMIN B COMPLEX

gallstones
hepatitis

liver problems
constipation
diarrhea
gastritis
ulcers
sore throat
strep throat
colds & flu
arthritis
broken bones
disc problems
nervousness
gout
low blood pressure
varicose veins
burns

VITAMIN B1 FUNCTION

to change glucose into energy or fat
memory vitamin
starch-sugar metabolism vitamin
resistance to noise & pain

SYMPTOMS OF LACK OF VITAMIN B1

feet and hands numb
lack of hydrochloric acid
low blood pressure
anemia
low metabolic rate
lactic acid buildup
pain — neuritis legs
water-clogged heart
sciatica
lumbago
neuralgia
starved thyroid
pain in knee
delayed ligament reflexes
nausea
slight paralysis
(approx. 50 mg. daily restorative)

VITAMIN B2 (Riboflavin) FUNCTION

brings oxygen to the eyes
milk sugar or lactose increases
need for B2 unless fat is
    adequate in diet

SYMPTOMS OF LACK OF VITAMIN B2

cracks at corners of mouth
    whistle lines
loss of upper lip
swollen eyelids
sensitive to light
eyelids itch and burn
watery eyes
poor night vision
bloodshot eyes
cataracts, glaucoma
blood vessels close to skin, red,
    as in alcoholics, etc.
bed sores
(approx. 150 mg. restorative)

144

    I knew of a baby whose parents had spent around $10,000 on hospital bills, because the baby could not use sugar, having diarrhea continually, and not having gained any weight in six (its first) months of life. The parents decided to help the baby on their own by giving it acidophilus culture, psyllium powder, raw goat's milk and honey, and fruits. Within two weeks the baby had gained from its six pounds nine ounces to almost ten pounds, its first weight gain. The last I heard, the child was doing well.

    In order for us to retain nourishment, Vitamin B6 is very important. Where it is not produced, as with this baby, acidophilus culture gives the body the necessary B6. The spyllium stops the diarrhea and heals the colon. Aloe vera is also useful for colon problems.

VITAMIN B6 (Pyridoxin) FUNCTIONS

Essential to use fatty acids,
    linoleic acids and amino
    acids from protein.
Assists in hormonal metabolism
    of thyroid.

Made in the colon (where colon is
sick, yogurt and acidophilus
culture are helpful to the
production of B6)

80% of the women on the "pill"
(contraceptive) are deficient
in B6 — also, usually becoming extremely nervous.
Could this be the cause of so
much cancer in the colon?

Wherever there is colitis or
cancer or shrunken colon
and related problems, B6 assists the healing process. The
stool will again become normal in size. It is my opinion
that B6 is better taken in a
tablet form for adults. It will
help also in eliminating
fluid.

SYMPTOMS OF LACK OF B6

eczema in babies
acne, psoriasis
skin dermatitis, wrinkles
fainting easily
sore mouth
muscle cramps
bed wetting
bladder retention
tooth decay
sinus problem
water retention
toxemia in pregnancy
hemorrhoids
ear noise
nausea in pregnancy — up to 250
    mg.
sea sickness, motion sickness —
    up to 250 mg.
irradiation sickness — to 250 mg.
neuritis from toxic condition
vomiting after operation
whooping cough

colitis, diarrhea
kidney stones
high cholesterol
epilepsy
neuritis from toxic condition
(approx. 50 mg. daily restorative)

B12 (Cyanocobalamin-Cobalt) FUNCTION

glands
phenobarbitol & Dilantin & heat
destroy folic acid. Folic acid
is necessary to use B12. This
is a good reason for using raw
cold-pressed oils and raw
fruits and nuts.
Essential in the use of meat protein
Essential to gland restoration,
where meat is used.

SYMPTOMS OF LACK OF B12

Inability to produce hydrochloric
acid
sore mouth, swollen tongue
bright red tongue, and painful
back stiffness and pain
menstural disturbances
spinal cord degeneration
muscle cramps
red scaley spots between nose &
lips
vaginal itching
eyelids painful & burning
loss of distance vision
(approx. 30 mg. restorative)

When Vitamin C. is taken in large doses for extended periods, such as
five to ten days, calcium and Vitamin B should be added, as the Vitamin
C leaches these elements and causes nervousness and hollow, easily-
broken bones.

There has been much discussion about Vitamin C. It has been my experience and the experience of many others that when Vitamin C is used (1,000 mg. an hour) in acute illness such as a cold, etc., it dissolves mucus and usually stops acute disease or inflammation within a day or two. It has been used successfully even with small babies.

Vitamin C has been considered to be harmful to the kidney when taken in high doses. Certainly it is when it is a coal tar product. Taking high doses of coal tar would be very harmful. To determine whether or not your Vitamin C is a coal tar product, you can make this experiment. Place the tablet or powder on a teaspoon with water, hold over the burner of the stove, and let boil. If it boils away to a white powder, it is not a coal tar product. If it boils to a sticky, black gum, it is a coal tar product. Vitamin C has recently been made from wood, and of course would be a synthetic. When made from corn and citrus, it is a natural food product. When used in case of a cold or acute disease, it should be determined just how the Vitamin C you use is made, or you will not get the results. Could this be the reason for the controversy about Vitamin C? I have found where acute disease is present, straight ascorbic acid is best, usually taking it only a day or two, as it dissolves mucus rapidly. Any acute disease brings with it rapid pulse, as waste is on the move in the blood. High doses of Vitamin C often increase the heartbeat, as with acute disease. The addition of approximately one capsule of cayenne will usually slow down and smooth out the heart. Bioflavinoid Vitamin C is best for daily dose.

With twenty-five 500-milligram tablets, liquefied with one-eighth cup warm water, each teaspoon will equal 1,000 milligrams; add honey to taste. Polio virus has been stopped in 72 hours with Vitamin C therapy. We have too long starved the diabetic of fruit sugars and accompanying Vitamin C which could stop the inflammation and running ulcers that seem to go with later stages of diabetes.

Vitamin C is actually an aid to saving the kidneys, as it keeps the mucus or inflammation from causing damate, dissolving the mucus and allowing it to pass through. Bright's Disease or any kidney damage is usually caused from a bad inflammation or acute disease with too much mucus passing through the kidneys, causing a break or damage. When used in conjunction with herbs for the kidneys, and where there has been previous damage, Vitamin C is not damaging to the kidneys as has been thought. It may also be interesting to note that you can start a forced elimination by taking high doses of Vitamin C, bringing on a cold.

VITAMIN C NECESSARY FOR

cell respiration
breaking down protein
healing
capillary
cartilage & connective tissue

VITAMIN C USEFUL IN

aspirin poisoning
snake bites
black widow spider bites
poison oak or ivy
carbon monoxide poisioning
radiation poisoning
broken bones
bruises
burns
poisonous bites

Useful in acute disease:
meningitis
encephalitis
virus disease
swollen glands
polio
asthma
respiratory
acute sinus
kidney infection
croup
nose bleeding
promotes blood clotting
metal poisoning
hay fever
colds
all virus disease (mumps,
     measles, chicken pox)
sore throat, strep
phlebitis
inflammation
swollen glands

SYMPTOMS OF LACK OF VITAMIN C

anemia
bleeding membrane
    (mouth, red toothbrush)
low blood pressure
nosebleed
loose teeth
edema
wounds will not heal
pigmentation during pregnancy
varicose veins
hepatitis, liver
cataracts
glaucoma
high blood pressure
ulcers
arthritis, gout
weakness in arteries
cold sores
adrenal exhaustion
rheumatic fever
high cholesterol
mononucleosis
disc problems

149

VITAMIN D NECESSARY FOR

phosphorus and calcium use
bones
teeth
growth

(People who do not get out in
the sunshine do themselves a
great injustice; much mental
illness is caused from lack of
calcium, and calcium cannot
be used without Vitamin D)

SYMPTOMS OF LACK OF VITAMIN D

high cholesterol
muscle cramps

broken bones
backache
pyorrhea
acne
nervousness
weakness
retarded growth
enlarged joints
bowed legs
faulty jaw development

VITAMIN E FUNCTIONS

reproduction vitamin
- anti-sterility
growth
nutrition
essential to use of A, C, D & K
protects fat tissue from abnor-
    mal breakdown (as in diabetes)
effective in menopause
effective in menstrual cramps
heart
blood pressure
effective on burns & scars
promotes clotting
healing broken bones
increases oxygen
destroyed by chlorine & chlorinated
        water — could be cause of some
        heart disease

VITAMIN E USEFUL IN

detached retina
premature babies
anemia
hernia
muscle weakness
crossed eyes
miscarriage
burns & scars
varicose veins

frostbite
pain
clots
phlebitis, diabetes
heart attack
thyroid gland
menopause syndrom
high cholesterol
stomach ulcers
elimination of poison
congenital heart
acne
cancer cell growth
skin cancer
hemophilia
sinus
arthritis
colitis
arterio sclerosis
gallstones
hepatitis
glaucoma
hemorrhoids
ulcers
hot flashes
broken bones
burns

VITAMIN B15 (Pangamic Acid)

Europe has Vitamin B15 on the market. It appears that American scientists and doctors have become so disenchanted with vitamins, they are not looking for any new ones.

VITAMIN H (Biotin) FUNCTIONS

Produced in the colon like B6
Some drugs & antibiotics kill
    the natural flora of the colon
    (friendly bacteria).

Present in the body in very
    small amounts.

SYMPTOMS OF LACK OF VITAMIN H

depression
hallucinations
panic

VITAMIN H NECESSARY FOR

Combatting:
    exzema
    dermatitis
    hair loss

VITAMIN K FUNCTIONS

Essential to clotting of blood.
Antibiotics interfere with synth-
    esis

SYMPTOMS OF LACK OF VITAMIN K

hemorrhages easily
hemophilia

152

VITAMIN B17 (Nitriloside)

It is thought that the lack of Vitamin B17 is a cause of cancer. It is thought that the addition of B17 kills cancer growths. When used in a shot form by a medical doctor, giving proof that it stops the growth of cancer, said doctor was put in jail. I understand he is one of those now treating cancer in Europe and Mexico. It has been proven by these men who treat cancer that the cancer can be killed with these methods. It is my opinion that many herbs used in known cancer formulas have a large amount of this factor. I also toy with the idea that it may be the parasites that are killing, as parasites living and multiplying on such refuse even during a fast will not release the mucus in which they reside. When certain herbs are taken and parasites killed, a healing crisis occurs, pouring forth the globs of mucus cancer tumors and whatever. While these men search for an individual factor to kill cancer, it may be well for them to consider a research into the herbs in these cancer formulas and the certain foods used in fasting for cancer, such as grapes. Nature has given us a broad field in which to search, and we have only scratched the surface, and that always under constant duress. We have too long looked for the individual factor; it is time we begin to look at the over-all plant substance and combinations of plants and herbs.

CALCIUM IS NECESSARY FOR

formation of teeth and bones
lactation & pregnancy
oxygen to brain
nerve impulse transmission
muscle contraction
promote clotting

CALCIUM IS USEFUL IN

pain
dental pain
delivery
broken bones
bites

SYMPTOMS OF LACK OF CALCIUM

menstural cramps
tooth decay
night sweats
leg cramps
mental depression
irritability
pre-menstural depression
fatigue
brooding, complaining
cyst formations
sores do not heal
lack of courage
soft bones
deterioration of spine
sleeplessness
nervousness
toe & leg cramps
muscle cramps

FLUORIDE IS NECESSARY FOR

promoting vitality

protecting against bone disease
strengthening bone, muscle
        and tendons
(The cabbage family is rich
        in fluoride.)

SYMPTOMS OF THE LACK OF FLUORIDE

varicose veins
brown spots on skin
eyeballs stick
liver trouble
yellow color
chapped hands
fear of dark
hard crust forms on nose
backwardness in manner

CHLORINE IS NECESSARY FOR

gastric secretions, digestion
regulating blood pressure & tissues
a body cleanser
present in salt

SYMPTOMS OF THE LACK OF CHLORINE

kidney, bleeding where no
        pathological changes exist
bloating
sluggish liver
mucus
hepatitis
high cholesterol
high blood pressure

CHOLINE FUNCTIONS

keeps arteries clear
(found in soy oil & wheat
    germ oil)

SYMPTOMS OF LACK OF CHOLINE

Without choline, cholesterol
    reaches high levels because it
    takes choline to produce
    lecithin. Damage to kidneys
    results from lack of choline
    when protein diet is used.

FOLIC ACID USEFUL IN

arteries
healing
use of Vitamin B12

SYMPTOMS OF LACK OF FOLIC ACID

pregnancy cap
skin dryness
joints dry
diarrhea
(approx. 50 mg. daily restorative)

IODINE IS NECESSARY FOR

regulating fluids
thyroid
aids nerves
anti-infection
mental energizer
produces thyroxin hormone
    which controls rate of oxygen
    utilization
sodium necessary for use of
    iodine
kelp or dulse (salt substitute)
    provides iodine & sodium
    (use up to 20 tablets daily; for
    more than 20 tabs., it is best
    to use kelp or dulse in liquid
    form)

SYMPTOMS OF LACK OF IODINE

myxedema
cretin
goiters
fatigue
lethargy (slow of mind)
loss of sex desire
low blood pressure
slowed pulse
weight gain on few calories
heart disease

155

thyroid cancer
high cholesterol
enlarged glands
always cold
dull pain under both shoulder
    blades
puffy face

IRON IS NECESSARY FOR

aids blood cells
development of tissue respira-
    tion
oxygen transportation

IRON FUNCTION

recycles except during menstrua-
    tion or hemmorhage
not absorbed without hydrocho-
    lin, or when taking alkalizing
    preparations
destroys Vitamin E — take 8
    hours apart

SYMPTOMS OF LACK OF IRON

cry involuntarily
lack oxygen
anemia
blood lacks color
decreased energy
weakness
dizziness
short breath
pounding heart
palpitations
fatigue
brittle fingernails with longitud-
    inal ridging, colorlessness
lacking vitality
forgetfulness
pain in heels
dull hearing
sleepless at night

SYMPTOM OF LACK OF IN-
OSITOL

hair loss

MAGNESIUM IS
NECESSARY FOR

preserving mineral balance
utilization of calcium

MAGNESIUM HELPFUL IN

heart surgery
broken bones
quickly neutralizes hydrochloric
acid in stomach
alcohol leaches magnesium
half as much magnesium as calcium used

SYMPTOMS OF LACK
OF MAGNESIUM

bed wetting
fear
grief apprehension
nervous indigestion
gas
palpitations
twitching muscles, eyes, etc.
muscle spasms
yellowish white in eyes
sensitive to noise
muscle ache and pain
insomnia
hyperactivity
convulsions
colitis
diarrhea
gastritis
kidney stones

157

dandruff
prostate gland problems
nervousness
backache
disc problems

TOO MUCH MAGNESIUM CAUSES

(as in laxative)
muscle weakness
slow heart
coma
unconsciousness
slow speech
drowsiness

MANGANESE FUNCTION

improving mental balance, poise,
    resistance & nerves
important in growth, pregnancy,
    lactation

158

NIACIN (Nicotine Acid, B3, Niacinamide)

High doses of niacin usually
    cause a hot flash which lasts
    only a short time but can be a
    rather frightening experi-
    ence. The more often niacin
    is taken, the less often the hot
    flash will occur. Niacin-
    amide will not cause the
    hot flash.

SYMPTOMS OF LACK OF NIACIN

eczema
confusion
depression
fatigue
fear
nervousness

neuralgia
canker sores
diarrhea
baby diarrhea
coated tongue
impaired memory
schizophrenia
tongue deep red with fissures —
fissures will turn black if
great deficiency, becomes
pellagra or the Black Tongue
Plague.

PHOSPHORUS NECESSARY FOR

Important for nursing mothers
Aids in development of cells
(bones & teeth)
Metabolism of fats
Necessary for mental power

SYMPTOMS OF LACK OF PHOSPHORUS

Afraid of tomorrow
dislike sex, work
fearful
general weakness
loss of muscle tone
numbness in limbs
prone to arthritis
paralysis

PABA (para amino benzoic acid)

Skin pigmentation (vitillige)
(approx. 1,000 mg. daily)
eczema
sunburn (approx. 1,000 mg. daily)
hair color restored (approx.
200 mg. after each meal)
Rocky Mtn. Spotted Fever (approx.
1,000 mg. daily)
Paba performs the same thing in
the body that sulfa drug does,
killing bacteria, without the
side effects of sulfa: extreme

fatigue, anemia, exzema. Paba makes sulfa ineffective, so the F.D.A. does not allow any food supplement furnishing more than 30 mg. without prescription.

PANTOTHENIC ACID NECESSARY FOR

lymph glands
adrenals
tonsils

SYMPTOMS OF LACK OF PANTOTHENIC ACID

hypoglycemia
exhaustion
blackouts
headache
nervousness
dizziness

digestive problems
depression
colitis
cataracts
low blood pressure
swollen glands
glaucoma
gastritis
ulcers
arthritis
gout
muscle cramps
stretch marks

PANTOTHENIC ACID HELPFUL IN

healing
    cold sores
    sinus
    asthma
    respiratory flu
    colds
(approx. 50-100 mg. per meal and
    at bedtime restorative—up to
    10,000 mg. daily is not toxic)
called anti-graying vitamin

PANCREATIN, PANCREATIC ENZYME

some vitamin products add this to their products, some are sold separately

used in pre-digestion of milk & other foods

digests protein & starch & cancer cells

in stomach, pancreatin destroyed by gastric juices. Digestive enzyme necessary — approx. 2 each meal. Pancreatin enzyme made from "armour zypanar" (pancreas of hog) meat. Product of usually ex-bile, pepsin, dehydrochloric acid, papain (papaya), diastaste (malt)

In my opinion, pancreatin in herb form is stillingia and all bitter herbs, which are preferrable to the animal products.

161

POTASSIUM NECESSARY FOR

regular heart action
normal growth
muscle control

SYMPTOMS OF LACK OF POTASSIUM

dropsy (edema)
paralysis
low blood sugar (hypoglycemia)
water retention
weak ligaments
listlessness
fatigue
constipation
soft flabby muscles
pulse weak, slow or irregular
heart attack or degeneration of muscle
swollen testicles or ovaries

foggy thinking
colon prolapsed
swollen ankles
dry throat
kidney damage
liver damage
bitter taste in mouth
inability to use sugar

Losses occur by

spilling off in urine
too much sodium intake
diuretics (water pills)
ATCH
cortisone
aspirin
drugs
alcohol
drinking too much water
vomitting
diarrhea
stress — excessive sugar causes stress, spilling off potassium. This could be more the cause of heart attack than too many fatty acids. Sugar decreases cell potassium, rendering heart and all muscles weak and flabby.
Another reason for heart weakness is the use of too much salt. If the intake is no more than 1 tsp. daily, at least 5,000 mg. of potassium is required. We Americans consume at least 1-5 tsps. of salt daily and do not eat enough fruits and vegetables to make up for the potassium deficiency.

SILICON NECESSARY FOR

natural alkalizer
regulating cell tissues

SILICON HELPFUL IN

drug addiction
aids nervous disorder

SYMPTOMS OF LACK OF SILICON

itchy ears
sties on eyes
ear discharge
ulceration of tongue
teeth sensitive
boils
nervous exhaustion
listlessness
no ambition for brain work

SODIUM NECESSARY FOR

natural alkalizer
regulating cell tissues
aiding nervous disorder

(Sodium is necessary when taking cortisone, or the result will be adrenal exhaustion. When taking licorice rather than cortisone, it is of no concern.)

SYMPTOMS OF LACK OF SODIUM

low blood pressure
heat stroke when in the sun too
    long
heat stroke symptoms:
    nausea
    dizziness
    exhaustion
    vomitting
    cramp of leg, back, or abdominal muscles being used at the time
    easy anger
    hair falling out
    loss of sense of smell
    indigestion
early morning exhaustion

SULPHUR NECESSARY FOR

toning blood

improving looks
stimulating liver secretions
making hair glossy
called the beautifying mineral

SYMPTOMS OF LACK OF SULPHUR

toxic condition (help elimination)
disc trouble
hair dull
joint troubles
joyless appearance
difficulty talking or singing
menstruation delayed
menstruation irregular
moodiness
sores do not heal
voicebox gives out easily

SUMPTOMS OF LACK OF ZINC

poor sexual development:
   Testicles & penis small
   no pubic hair
   addition of zinc will bring on
      development of external
      genitalia
   for severely burned persons
   prostate gland problems

(approx. 200 mg. zinc sulfate 3
   times daily restorative)

CHAPTER SIX

IRIDOLOGY — THE EYES ARE THE WINDOWS OF THE BODY

You have heard it said, "The eyes are the windows of the soul." The eyes are also the windows of the body. The change I have watched in the eyes, like a kaleidoscope as the body begins to heal, is a marvel of beauty and wonder. The reason medical science does not accept iridology as a true science is because their drugs do not heal the body and they cannot experience this beautiful change in the eye as repair is made. If they were to use nature's methods, they would soon learn, as I have, that the eye is a wonderful x-ray and that God did not place us here on earth all closed in so the only way we could find out what was wrong was either to be cut open or to have all kinds of fluids run through our veins so we could be photographed. No, He put windows on us. It has been evident to many who have learned about iridology that with the use of herbs and mild foods, the eye changes as health is being restored. You can see in the eye the places where the bones have been broken. You can see where surgery has been performed. You can see which glands are functioning and which ones are not. You can determine if there are parasites and where in the body they have settled. You can see when the person has taken drugs and where in the body they are lodged. You can see the vitality, strength, or weakness of the individual body. You can see if there is anemia or an over-toxic condition. You can see accumulations of waste as in cancer tumors, arthritis, etc. You can see if the body is nervous, and you can determine just how nervous by the number of nerve rings on the eye. You can see, also, the inherently weak places in the body, where it is most likely to break down and when it does break down.

People have said, "That sounds impossible. How could it possibly work? What could possibly cause the problem to show up on the eyes?" Man has devised an oscilloscope. This instrument, when hooked electrically to a car or many other electrical, mechanical devices, will show traces on a TV screen of the actual electrical impulses in the car or machine, allowing the engineer or mechanic to tell exactly how it is functioning or to detect any malfunction. It will show any weak or strong impulses. It will also show exactly the rhythmical speed or timing of the machine. Man has also attached sensing devices to the body of an astronaut, and after sending him thousands of miles into outer space, information is telemetered back to mission control for doctors to observe. We can tell his pulse rate, blood pressure, body temperature, respiration, and general body condition. We can determine when he exercises, his strength, and his endurance by these telemetering devices. It was only twenty years or so ago when chiropractors were thrown into jail and labeled as quacks for the use of electrical, diagnostic devices. Today, you can walk into any hospital and see such devices attached, with the addition of needles, to patients; and in the nursery this research appears to be cruel and brutal, especially when it has to be accompanied by all the antibiotics necessary to keep down infection resulting from the needles. Some parents have paid out thousands of dollars in hospital and doctor bills, while this experimenting was going on with their babies, the antibiotic and all drugs slowing down and even inhibiting the process of healing. If it is possible for man to make such devices, is it not just possible that God, in his infinite wisdom, could have put a screen on us that made it unnecessary to go through all the pain of tests. The eyes are literally the oscilloscopes of the body and much, much more. When medical science learns how to heal the body of chronic disease, they will learn that this is true.

In my discussion of iridology I will not go into any really extensive study. My intention is to show you some of the main things to look for and some discoveries that I have found, that others have not, so you will be able to make enough of an analysis of your own body to help yourself with herbs, vitamins, etc.

Some of the weak places showing on the eye you may be born with; some are caused by injury; others we will just call weakness, acquired by either a flaw in personal character, choice, or environment. They all show up in the same way; and since this analysis study has nothing to do with the physique, you will not be able to determine which of the four is the cause in anyone but possibly yourself. Personality character weakness that causes illness I will show in somewhat of an outline form to help you to understand.

I. Inherent weakness (causes illness)
   (most dangerous)
   A. Heart
   B. Liver
   C. Kidney
   D. Glands

     Many weaknesses are related or interrelated and move along in the body like a chain reaction. Some weaknesses are unrelated, and there are times when a person can live to a ripe old age with a lot of weaknesses that never connect. The inherent, inborn, kind of weakness, we can sometimes change by diet and correct living. The person inherently very weak cannot get away with the abuse that a more healthy person could give his body. Inherent weakness shows up in this way:

1)

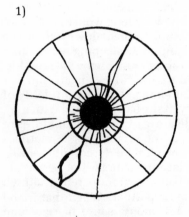

Bowed out place

2)

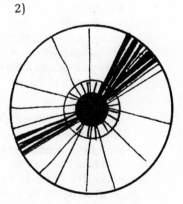

Deeper shadow

II. Personality weakness (causes illness)
    A. Too sensitive (self pity)
    B. Not sensitive enough (doesn't care about self or others)
    C. Rebellious, stubborn (too destructive)
    D. Weak willed — this person who allows others to do his deciding often accepts wrong choice in diet
    E. Indecisive — person who can't make up his mind, usually will go the middle of the road
    F. Negative, pessimistic, or worrying type
    G. Inability to give or receive love
    H. Unable to accept things as they are — there are those who know that if they had made the world, they would have done things differently, so are never able to quite accept things, the world, or other people as they are.
    I. Inferiority complex
    J. The idealist — It is with difficulty that the idealist lives with weakness or imperfection, in himself or in his fellowmen. To begin with, as he grows up he believes hopefully in himself and everyone. As he becomes disappointed in others or himself and his weakness, he is shattered. When those he loves and respects disappoint him, he can become very ill, at times causing a nervous breakdown or possibly death. I knew a young woman with very high ideals who had a complete breakdown when she discovered that her husband was sleeping with other women. She was unable to accept him on the basis of this, even though she loved him with all her heart, but her standards did not lower far enough to allow infidelity of any kind, let alone adultery. If she had remained with him, it could have killed her. Healthwise it is better for birds of a feather to flock together, as the saying goes. Sometimes those of idealistic temperament, who do not quite measure up themselves, will place the standard of perfection on some other person — a parent, a grandparent, a church leader, a friend, or a business partner. When that friend falls, their whole world, testimony, sense of right and wrong, love and forgiveness, suddenly crashes about their feet.

There are those who wish to achieve greatness; but because of a parent's bad example or the circumstances in which they have found themselves, they are never quite sure how much of that parent's traits have been handed down to them. They do not quite ever believe they can make it. They either become resigned to living with mediocrity or they are continually torn. There have been many parents who have had to live out the rest of their lives with broken health or have gone to an early grave because a wayward child has broken their hearts and spirits. Where along this road to perfection can we find a place of health? We have been commanded,

> "Be ye therefore perfect, even as your
> Father which is in heaven is perfect."

We are not commanded to make sure our brother is perfect but only to forgive seventy times seven. David O. McKay said something that may be helpful: "Be tough on yourself but tender with others." Surely there is nothing wrong with being an idealist. The great things that have been done in all generations of time have been accomplished by the idealist. Where then can we look for an eventual peaceful reign but with those who strive for perfection? Where can we fit in all this seeking after perfection? Are we a help or a hindrance to the progress of man? Somewhere, the wisdom of reality must temper idealism into love, Godlike love. Deep, real love often takes a lifetime of living to develop. It can bring with it the calm, peaceful, harmonious beauty of the well-mellowed aged. When this wisdom is never learned, if patience and true love is never found, there can be no peace of soul — only the tormented pain that accompanies the unaccepted reality that life and people are not perfect. In this way, the idealist, for all his striving, has missed the mark he set so high; and his punishment is self-destruction. What a waste. If we could only vaguely see the faults of others, enough to recognize those poor characteristics we would not want to make a part of us, we could then make a beginning. It is a sorry fact that some peoples' whole lives would be a total waste, except that they can serve as a bad example. We could also become so trusting of others as to set a trap for the weak man's dishonesty, thus contributing to his downfall. It would help if we could see and be aware without hate, yet still never give anyone a chance to cheat us or steal from us. The Lord has given us some good advice when He said, "Be as wise as serpents, yet as harmless.

169

III. Choice weakness (causes sickness)
    A. Constantly making wrong choices and often for the wrong reasons
    B. Rebellious
    C. Stubborn

D. Must have own way, no matter what — right or wrong, will eat the cake, drink the liquor, smoke the cigarette, even if it kills them, and it usually does.
E. Undecided
F. Weak willed — unable to change even when a better way is known
G. Wrong diet as a child — there are many parents, had they known, who would have fed their children much better; and because they did not, the child has developed weakness, chronic disease, and a taste for many wrong foods.
H. Use of drugs — there are also those who learn a better way who wish they had never allowed the destruction of drugs to enter their bodies, but the damage has been done; drugs still remaining in the body can be removed by herbs and mild foods, but often the damage they have done can never be repaired.

IV. Environmental Weakness

A. Child (too much or too little control) An example: artistic, sensitive, or mechanical child not being able to express his own personality type because of parents of a different type not being able to understand. I do not believe, however, that a just God would place his children only according to their obedience or lack of obedience in a world before coming here. Besides what was merited in the pre-existence, I feel he would surely place each of us in the very best soil so as to develop to our advantage. As much as I love plants and flowers, and as far below the nature of God as is my place, I would not put my house plants out in the snow. People we love who are different from ourselves have a way of giving us some polish, if we can look at it that way. Gibby said,

> "When life becomes a grind remember it is
> only a test to see whether you'll come
> out broken or polished."

Many circumstances in which we find ourselves by birth are just that: Often the people we love or hate around us in our own families help to shape and grind out our personalities. At times those we love the most can also be our destroyers. Oliver Wendell Holmes said it very well:

"There is almost always at least one key to this side-door. This is carried for years hidden in a mother's bosom. Fathers, brothers, sisters and friends, often, but by no means so universally, have duplicates of it. The wedding ring conveys a right to one; alas if none is given with it.

"Be very careful to whom you trust one of these keys of the side-door. The fact of possessing one renders those even who are dear to you very terrible at times. You can keep the world out from your front-door, or receive visitors only when you are ready for them; but those of your own flesh and blood, or of certain grades of intimacy, can come in at the side-door, if they will, at any hour and in any mood. Some of them have a scale of your whole nervous system, and can play all the gamut of your sensibilities in semitones – touching the naked nerve-pulps as a pianist strikes the keys of his instrument. I am satisfied that there are as many great masters of this nerve-playing as Vieuxtemps or Thalberg in their lines of performance. Married life is the school in which the most accomplished artists in this department are found."

Too many times we give the keys to the doors of our heart to the wrong person.

B. Young adult (too much control, too little control, wrong diet, lack of love, or lack of spiritual faith). Young people trying their wings make many mistakes that will scar them for life, physically as well as spiritually.

C. Marriage
   1. Too much control by one person
   2. Not able to express self
   3. Wrong diet — There are times when one partner insists inadvertently on killing the other. I knew a man who was given up to die of cancer, who went for help to a health resort and, after receiving all the information on diet, returned home only to have his wife say, "If you are going to eat all that rabbit food you will have to fix it yourself." The man is now dead. This happens so often when one of the partners sees the truth of natural methods and the other partner stubbornly refuses to allow them to do it, thus contributing to the demise of their loved one.

  4. Lack of love

  5. Lack of faith — infidelity

D. Poor air (fallout)

E. Poor living conditions (unsanitary)

F. Cannot resolve life with physical or personality surroundings — There are times when one partner wants an entirely different atmosphere than the other party, causing a constant conflict, inwardly or outwardly, either way causing illness in the person unable to resolve his or her life to the immediate surroundings. Nothing is stopping the person from getting out of the situation. If a person chooses to remain, he must bring himself into harmony with his partner in order to be well in his environment. We must be equally balanced socially, intellectually, spiritually, and physically in order to be well. Many a great genius has hardly found time to eat. The imbalanced life of the professor in the intellectual has caused the jokes about the absent-minded professor; or we see the beautiful physical body exercised to the limit, walking around on display with an empty head on its shoulders; or there is the social outcast who never ever learns how to relate to his fellow creatures. There are some, also, who become so involved in the spiritual that they wish they were dead, often neglecting the necessities and essentials, not recognizing that all these things are relative to health as well as happiness.

G. War

H. Famine

I. Lack of achievement, or making progress — This is an individual who suffered much illness by environmental weakness. We must all have a sense of achievement in one direction or another, setting goals and reaching them.

J. Life in general

  1. Poison in water, food, chemicals, additives

  2. Those who do not ever seem to know when or how to rest and relax — they just go and go until they drop, because of the many demands of a fast-moving society. Sooner or later, these externally or internally caused weaknesses in character or our surroundings show up on the eye in relation to the damage they have done in our being. We have heard a great deal in the past few years about the power of positive thought. The average person is fairly well-converted to the belief that if we want to have anything we must think positively. At times, the mind may be sick because the body is sick. At other times, the body becomes ill from negative thoughts, sometimes a little of both. It is my firm belief that it is difficult to say which came first, the

chicken or the egg — was it mind or body that caused mental or physical illness. It is also my belief that if you lived in constant fear of cancer because one of your parents died of cancer, you would eventually die of the disease, drawing it to you like a magnet. Job said,

Job 3:25 *"For the thing which I greatly feared is come upon me, and that which I was afraid of it came unto me."*

To help you analyze the problems in your body, looking into your own windows, the next thing to look for is an accumulation of waste in any given area. It has been found that these are the areas connected to each part of the body. Shown only in general,

3)

Right Eye

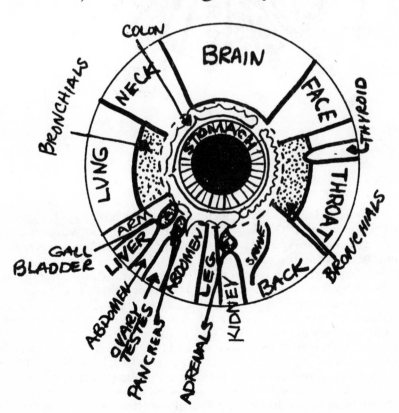

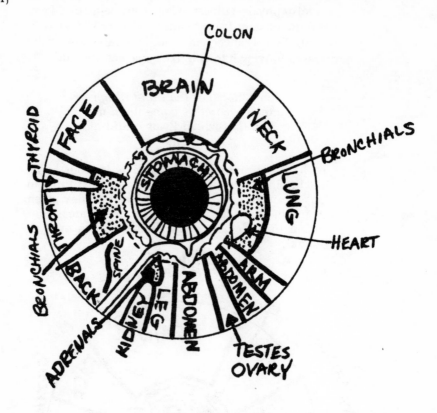

Left Eye

When one lady asked her doctor about all the brown spots appearing on her eyes he said, "Oh, those are just freckles." The brown spots he saw only as freckles are spots that gradually appear on the eye in a given area directly, showing the same area in the body where chronic waste has settled. The darker the spot or area, the more chronically deteriorated it is. As the body begins to heal, the spot becomes lighter, and even whiter, around the outside edge of the spot. The spot gradually gets lighter and smaller until it fades to white and then is gone. When this has happened to a person they did not have to look in the mirror and say, "I am well." They had been getting well all along, and they knew it. To give you a few examples of what I feel are the main things to look for will be sufficient for this book. There are books listed in my bibliography which you can use to make an extensive study if you wish. My studies have not come entirely from books, but from personal observation and experience.

5)

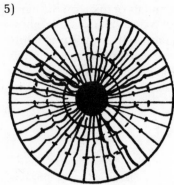

Nerve ring extending all the way around; this person is ready for a nervous breakdown.

6)

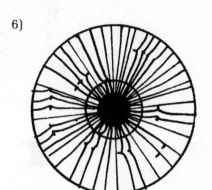

Nerve ring may show up only in places where there is tension.

175

7)

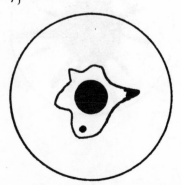

You can tell as well as an x-ray exactly how the colon looks — if it is impacted in places, distended, or if it is chronically sick.

Any white in the iris of the eye indicates mucus or toxin on the move in the blood acute inflammation. Any brown or black spots show chronic illness. The eye of a child with leukemia will show up so white as to be almost void of color. They literally suffocate in their own mucus in the blood that will not eliminate from the body; adding blood only compounds the problem.

8)

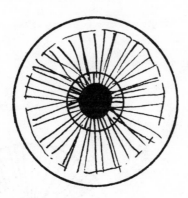

Shows sodium or drug ring; sometimes will only appear in one area, not all the way around, showing the place where drugs have settled, a grey-white ring around the outside edge.

176

9)

Anytime there is a sunburst, deep, dark lines, this reveals parasites in the body in the place shown. A diabetic's eyes usually look like this with toxic colon and pancreas. As herbs are taken to kill the parasites, the lines will begin to gradually disappear.

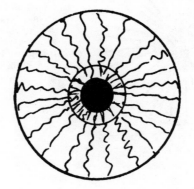

Where lines are wavy rather than straight it shows that the glands are out of balance.

11)

If a spot appears on the particular gland, this is usually the cause. If the lines are only wavy and no spots show, it is always adrenal (stress).

If herbs are taken and the spot goes away with lines remaining wavy, stress is still causing too much work on the adrenals. The only other thing I need to mention would be to help you see vitality:

12)

Where lines are straight and clearly in focus, this shows strength — usually shows in youth. Where texture is fine, shows good, inherent body. It is possible in this type to find chronic brown spots, indicating poor choice in diet.

13)

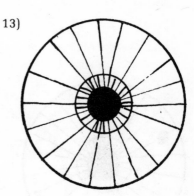

If texture is loosely woven, inherent weakness.

178

14)

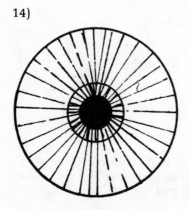

Where lines are watery and flat as if not in focus, even if texture is fine, this shows weakness. Eyes usually look like this in old age. The body may be clear of chronic disease and fine textured and yet weakness of body shows in this way.

For example, I knew a man whose eyes were clear — no chronic disease; he was injured as a young man in the neck and head and in later life in a car accident had an injury to the head which caused a stroke and made him blind in one eye. Because of faith, his sight was restored; but due to the damage to the brain, gradual paralysis began to take place until he died, due to the lack of brain strength and ability to perform body functions. He had lived all his life suffering weakness, so lived always as he knew he must, on a better-than-average diet. Those who have heard him preach health and natural foods could say, "He is gone and I am still here and I didn't have to eat all that health stuff." The interesting thing about his death was that he suffered no pain. He had no bad odor or bad breath, as his body was really quite clear and clean of poisons. You may hear a man brag once in a while who says this: "I've smoked and drank all my life; I'm 85 years old and never had a sick day." That man was blessed with an inherently strong body. What magnificent health he could have had had he obeyed the rules of health. We see often in families where nutrition is extremely poor, all members seem to do all right on it until suddenly one will come along who is weak, as if all the bad blood of generations were dumped into that one sickly body. This one will die on the same diet that the remainder of the family can be sustained on. There are people, as has been said, who cannot survive on what society today calls a well-rounded diet. Because of the poor, poisoned, adulterated, chemical foods upon which we have tried to subsist, there are more and more of these people who cannot survive.

179

15)

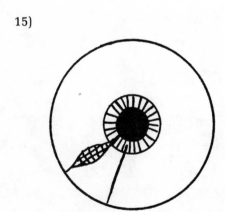

Healing knits like this and finally closes into a straight line.

It has been said, "A little knowledge is a dangerous thing." What little I have taught you here will be helpful in that you can determine chronic disease. You have already learned there is only one disease. What you may decide by way of analysis of your eyes will not matter much except where the glands are concerned. Hopefully what you see will encourage you to start a cleansing program. If and when you do, the magic that takes place in your eyes will make a believer of you. Gregor Mendel said, "To know what to ask is to already know half." Leo Hebraeus, a famous physician in Genoa and Naples wrote,

> "Intellectual beauty – the beauty of order, plan, and harmony – is superior to physical beauty, the supreme beauty is the order, plan and harmony of the universe, which is the outward expression of divine beauty; love rises in stages from admiration and pursuit of physical to intellectual to heavenly beauty and culminates in the intellectual love of God – the understanding and appreciation of the cosmic order and a desire to be united with diety."

The wonder of the human body is a masterpiece in harmony. The wonder and beauty I have beheld in the eyes has turned my amazement into a vibrant solid reality of the truth that the eyes are the windows of the body.

CHAPTER SEVEN
THE HORMONE BALANCE

Nature's Own Insulin

Natural-Type Cortisone

Natural Estrogen

Natural ATCH

Natural Thyroid

There are two main types of diabetes, thin diabetes (le diabete maigre) and the fat type (le diabete gras). The first type usually occurs in children and young people. The second type usually relates to the imbalance of the glands as a person grows older, becoming more obese and toxic, sometimes causing a deterioration of the pancreas where the hormone insulin is produced. We have often seen a sudden unexplained diabetes develop in a child or young person, or often the child is born with the damage to the pancreas; but where there has been no original damage, I have made an interesting discovery. I feel it is important for me to let it be known. When the child seems to develop diabetes early and suddenly, it is my opinion that the parasites, samonella or trichinosis, usually beginning growth in the small intestine and spreading eventually through the entire body, become deeply embedded as to entirely fill the pancreatic gland, more particularly the island of Langerhans. The adult trichinosis lives about six weeks. During this life span, one female produces 1,500 larvae. These larvae are carried by the blood and become lodged in the capillaries of any organ or tissue of the body. They have been found in all organs of the body, even in milk of nursing mothers, thereby being transmitted to the nursing child. Children and young people acquire these parasites from any or all of these causes, from the mother before birth, from mother's milk, incorrect mucus diet, unclean surroundings, or bad chicken or pork. It is my opinion that this explains why very young children develop diabetes. It has been previously thought that it was hereditary, but not in this way. It has been my interesting observation that when these parasites are killed by using certain herbs, the accumulated mucus upon which they feed will be expelled during a healing crisis. The interesting thing which also occurs at this time is that the eye changes as the toxic waste is moved and the parasites are killed.

You will recall that I said the eye of a diabetic has dark spokes reaching out from a toxic colon area like a sunburst and heavily occupying the pancreas area of the eye. As the body heals and cleans, as parasites are killed, the deep cut lines begin to gradually disappear, and the test tape begins to lose the green color until finally no more green shows at all. The wasting stops and a fine tone appears again on the flesh.

Parasites cannot take hold unless the body is overly encumbered with toxic waste due to incorrect diet or inherent weakness, such as slow metabolism, low blood pressure, etc. Neither can parasites nor germs live on healthy, sound tissue. We do not have maggots on our sink or in our garbage cans, because we keep them clean. The body is in a constant state of trying to return us to dust at the slightest provocation. Whenever there is waste matter which is not expelled from the body, we will find food for parasites and germs. If the body were maintained at a sound and completely nourished state in which all body wastes were burned or expelled, there would be no need to fear the microbe nor his undesirable cousins.

Many people live in a half-decayed state and do not recognize it, other than to know that they do not feel well. Nature has already done in their bodies a great deal of her work before the body is laid in the ground. It is interesting to note that trichinosis is so conspicuously absent in the middle east where little or no pork is used, due to the religious laws of the Jewish and Islamic faiths. With these parasites crying for more of the kinds of foods they can thrive on, continually calling to the person in whose body they have taken up residence, it seems to the person that he cannot get enough candy, cake, and goodie junk in general. The hunger for sweets is unbearable, so he promptly obeys the call of his now well-associated friends and gives them what they want, thus giving them food to grow upon and propogate their young. This cycle continues until the diabetic state (if the parasites have invaded the pancreas sufficiently), fast approaching the beginning of a disease he will live with from then on, until it is evetually his executioner.

Medical science has supposedly come to the rescue, with fanfare; the discoverers being knighted and given the Nobel Prize. To an extent, they have prolonged the patient's life, provided he is a very methodical and remarkably organized individual, so as to be accurate in his analysis of each symptom as it occurs and to take exactly the amount of insulin required.

At the time F. G. Banting and C. H. Best discovered that the body would accept the hormone (as it was named) of animal and use it as if the person himself had produced it, there was no exact knowledge of the principles of the chemical nature of internal secretion. It was a great discovery; and many discoveries have been added since this doorway of new knowledge has been opened to our view: cortisone, thyroid, ACTH, estrogen, testosterone, etc.; however, nothing for the diabetic to effect a cure, but rather a promise of continued life as long as insulin is available to the user. Shots continually and a careful diet: this would be his status for the rest of his life.

People who are ill and unable to take food in a normal way are often given glucose solution directly into the blood, which would tend again to prove Professor Ehret's theory that it is grape sugar (glucose), not protein, that builds the body. We know that even glycogen (a polysaccharide animal starch) is derived in the body from glucose, especially found in liver and muscles, and that another change takes place to change grape sugar (glucose) into glycogen, which proves that it is grape sugar (glucose), not protein, which maintains; and fats also must be changed into glucose before being used, with hormones stimulating the glands to bring it about. It is my conclusion once more that, as Professor Ehert has stated, it is grape sugar or glucose which is fuel for the human body. This is the reason fruit is a superior food.

183

Hormones are essential to allow proper change of fats, proteins, complex sugars and starches into glucose. It is my opinion that when insufficient hormone is secreted into the body from any or all glands, the body becomes toxic (which, of course, it can become due to wrong combinations and non-nutritious toxin-forming foods), and fats and undigested protein and starches remain in the blood as cholesterol or hardened fat (overweight). In this sense, both starches and sugars are turned into fat. The opposite occurs in some cases of diabetes when sufficient insulin hormone to make the change from protein and starch and complex sugars to simple sugar or glucose are used. If natural, simple sugars of fruit, so as to cuase less change to take place, are used, it is easier on the already sick body; however, it is still necessary to have enough insulin hormone to effect the utilization of the glucose in maintaining the body until it becomes clean. When sugar spills off into the urine and is not used, the body will waste away.

With the exception of where there has been organic damage, the first thing to bring about a cure would be to remove the cause (the parasite), having sufficient insulin or the herb insulin to maintain the body until the glands begin to produce again. There is a problem as I see it with the pancreatic drug insulin. (It should really not be called a drug as it is from the animal pancreas.) The problem is that it has a tendency to add toxic protein waste; and because of the nature of the drug, even natural sugars are excluded or cut to low amount in the diet when these are the foods the diabetic so desperately needs to maintain a sound, healthy body. In fact, Banting and Best have themselves proven to the world that without sufficient sugar, the body wastes and dies. In 1925 Professor Arnold Ehret, in his book *Mucusless Diet Healing System*, gave his theory:

> "High protein foods act as stimulation for a certain time because they decompose at once in the human body into poison."[1]

There are, of course, minerals, vitamins, and sugars to be drawn from the meat, but a change must be made in the meat by the body in order to be used; because it is of such a toxic nature, it must be eliminated very rapidly after making this change, or it becomes poisonous to the body. It is well-known that animal substances begin to deteriorate much more rapidly at death than does plant life after being picked. This deterioration takes place in meats much faster also when exposed to high temperature so it is put under refrigeration immediately to keep from being the cause of dreaded food poisoning. Plant life, on the other hand, is able to be hauled a good distance and kept for some time in the hot sun. We see fruit sitting out in the hot sun at a fruit stand, and I have seen truckloads of oranges or melons piled high out in the open, hot, Phoenix August sun, 115 degrees, on their way to market.

Another interesting thing about fruits and vegetables is that for a certain time, they do better without refrigeration. Once refrigerated and then taken out, they deteriorate very rapidly, as if something were killed or broken down. Those who contest that meat is a superior food should note the definite physiological difference between vegetable products and those of flesh foods. In the vegetable kingdom the constructive forces combine inorganic materials with inorganic water and organic

184

---

[1]This means generally high protein foods such as meat. Soy bean is a vegetable protein, but is still too high for a mild food diet.

seed, sun, and air, changing them into a complex organic organism, storing all minerals, vitamins, enzymes, organic life within its tissues. The forces go only to make a strong or a weak plant, depending upon the nutrients in the soil. In the animal kingdom, however, it is different, in that the constructive and destructive forces are going on simultaneously. Waste products must be quickly eliminated, or the destructive forces get ahead of the constructive ones. The minute a creature is dead, the deterioration of protein begins immediately. It has already begun as the animal is dying, this is why we cannot eat anything that has died of itself. Vegetables, fruits, and nuts are made up of certain proteins but are far more durable. It takes a great deal of heat, man-made, to break them down. In other words, meat products are of a more unstable composition: they require a sound hormone balance to be changed in the body. The only reason it has been supposed they are a better source of protein than vegetables is that they are more concentrated and because they, by first appearance, break down more quickly. Could this be because they are already in the process of decomposition? Actually they do not break down as rapidly as vegetables and fruits, as has been shown, taking four to six hours to change for use as fuel. You may argue, "What about old people who cannot chew vegetables, etc? They must surely be broken down in cooking." Raw vegetable juice is the answer to bring back the vital life force through the vitality of live, raw food. As this vitality is restored, the body will be able to accept these foods readily. It is recognized that the hormone insulin, when produced by the body, is a protein molecule. By the same method, a mother producing milk for her baby, when living on nothing but fruit, can produce protein milk as I have told you I did. Richer protein milk is not produced by eating meat and in most cases, I would even say it is not as rich. It is interesting to note that a diabetic or any person who has an imbalance of the adrenal, thyroid, pituitary, hormone, etc., has the inability to digest meat at all in the later stages of disease; and the reason why so many are considered terminal is that they can no longer tolerate meat. What a crime. What an insane concept is the high protein theory. For my part, I am convinced that an herb insulin would be superior to an animal insulin. I am convinced that the new chemical insulins are causing the diabetic to look worse and worse. This of course is only my opinion; you will have to find this answer for yourself.

In diabetes, you may argue, the person afflicted often becomes nauseated when eating any fruit, as in pancreatitis when inflammation is manifest by local tenderness or swelling. As soon as the parasites are killed by means of herbs, any sign of pancreatitis will disappear, and fruit will be tolerable. The herbs I have found to contain insulin, and I am sure there are others if a search were made, are goldenseal, and cedar or juniper berries, the latter being the most potent. The interesting facts about both of these herbs are their other qualities. They are both helpful in kidney problems; they kill germs; they act as a tonic and cleanser. Some of the herbs that kill parasites are pumpkin seed (and it is the best), sage, senna, garlic, sorrel, tansey, vervain, buckthorn bark, heal all. There are herbs that will assist the dead parasites to move out of the body. Goldenseal and juniper are in this class, also blue violet and many others. Formulas and home remedies are listed in the chapter on herbs.

In the second type, the fat type, insulin production may be inadequate because of the destruction of islets of Langerhans tissue by chronic inflammatory disease. More commonly, however, no such lesions are present, and the cause of this type is called idiopathic. Medical writers of pathology have decided upon this word idiopathic, meaning, according to the dictionary, "a disease not caused or preceeded by any other primary disease." I do not believe in such a thing as an idiopathic disease. It is my opinion that all disease has a cause. It seems to me the word idiopathic is used for lack of an accurate knowledge of the real cause so is left as the dictionary further states, "peculiar to individual, a suffering disease."

186

Diabetes is found more commonly in persons who overeat, where the islets have been thought to have become gradually diseased. It is my opinion that the cause of this type of diabetes is related to any or all of these causes: mucus-forming food; lack of exercise; an accumulation of mucus in the pancreas, making fertilized soil for parasites; too much consumption of sugar (sucrose), calling on the pancreas to produce more and more insulin to change the sucrose to simple sugar so it can be used by the body, all in all causing a breakdown in the pancreas' ability to produce insulin. Long periods of overeating sugar and starch products until glycosuria, or spilling off of sugar, state is reached. This fat type in the beginning, where no lesions are present, can be temporarily cured by merely reducing the intake of sucrose sugar; eventually, however, the weakness and disease is on its way.

Use of herbs and correct diet brings this type much more quickly into a normal state. I feel also that there can be an over-stress situation, causing a draining of the adrenal glands which may cause this type to want more and more sugar, as fatigue and weakness calls for sugar to bring them up out of the so-called low blood sugar slump. I feel some causes may be found in adrenal or pituitary malfunction, resulting even in the desire to overeat, as there is always an extreme nervousness involved with the diabetic.

In the discussion of diabetes, we must talk about sugar; glucose sugar (chemical formula $C6H12O6$) is about half as sweet as cane sugar. We call it dextrose or grape sugar. It is the sweetness we taste in fruit, seeds, leaves, flowers, honey, and roots. Glucose is also found in the bodies of men and animals (the cause of the sticky sweetness of blood). Glucose is a sugar which does not need to be digested. When taken into the body, molecules or particles of glucose pass directly through the walls of the small intestines, the place from which all nourishment is absorbed into the bloodstream.Glucose carried into the blood oxidizes to supply heat and energy to all of the body. Sugar turns to fats and to muscle. A pig does not get fat from being fed fats; he gets fat eating corn.

All other carbohydrates and all sugars of a complex nature must be broken down by digestion into this simple grape sugar or glucose before they can be utilized by the body. It has been proven that normally indigestible cellulose found in vegetables breaks into glucose by intestinal bacterial action.

In the normal person glucose makes up to 0.1% of the blood, and in the diabetic the amount of glucose in the blood is increased and is spilled off unused into the urine. The body wastes, which would indicate the requirement of the use of glucose sugar needed to live. Glucose is given directly into the veins when a person is unable to take food.

In the case of diabetes it may be questioned, could I live on glucose sugar in the veins, as is done in the hospital intravenous feeding?

When glucose is used, antibiotics are usually necessary after the first few days to stop infection, because medical science does not understand that the moment the person goes into a fasting state the body begins to eliminate waste, causing the acute infections that occur while taking only intravenous feeding.

It has been assumed that it is the lack of protein, because as soon as protein is eaten the elimination stops. When a person cannot take protein, it is thought that the lack of protein caused the protein deterioration that accompanies an overwhelming elimination of toxic waste into the blood.

For the diabetic it is usually necessary to have extra insulin to utilize sucrose sugars and starches so as to make the change to simple glucose sugar. This is the reason why most diabetics can eat fruit or honey without insulin as long as starches are not eaten in the same meal. This is why they could take glucose in the veins, but here again the body will begin its fasting elimination. When the body arrives at a serious stage of elimination the person often dies of pneumonia or infection unless antibiotics are administered. As the toxic waste moves into the blood causing a heavy obstruction to bodily functions and when in a weakened condition the waste cannot be moved out, death usually follows. The body's protein begins its deterioration process as death proceeds in its course to end life. When this deterioration reaches a certain point death occurs.

If the body were clean and free from waste it could continue for extended periods on glucose in the veins. There is another factor, however, indispensable after a while to strength, which is a part of the creation of fuel heat and energy. The breakdown of bulk which causes combustion has a real part in the continuance of life, but it does not have to be protein bulk adding only more toxic waste to the already sick body, unable to accurately make necessary changes. Does this give hope to the terminally diseased person? Yes, it does when it is understood.

It should be mentioned that there are some cases of diabetes where insulin in the blood is higher than non-diabetics, indicating to me that there is a failure of the mechanism binding insulin in the plasma. this is an observation in cases usually of a mature nature. This indicates to me also that the person had a hypoglycemic condition prior to the onset of diabetes causing the constant over demand for insulin, bringing on the insulin shock and resultant low blood sugar slump. In a fasting state most insulin remains bound to a substance part of the plasma. As soon as glucose is given, bound insulin disappears rapidly and unbound insulin increases moving out in the blood to prepare for use. This should tell us that there is even a certain function connected to insulin affecting the use of glucose. As I see it there are two definite parts: one to change sucrose and starch to glucose, and another to utilize glucose. In most cases it is only the first. In giving intravenous feedings, the insulin must be kept at a correct level and acid must be brought down to alkaline and also infection (or elimination) must be kept down. A very complicated touch and go situation.

Now if there were herbs that could normalize all factors this would be a great advantage. The interesting thing about the insulin-type herbs is that this is exactly what they do; the same way kelp works on either hypo or hyper thyroid.

There are several kinds of imbalance in the hormones of the body, so complex and interrelated that it is with difficulty sometimes that we can separate them into a single need, as each lack or inability to produce the hormones related to a particular gland has an effect on the others. We call one diabetes, another Cushing's Disease, another Addison's Disease, also diseases related to the thyroid and genital organs not producing adequately. We single out as a definite disease the one which causes death the quickest. Diabetes is the first on the list, as you can die quicker of the lack of insulin than from the lack of adrenal, cortin, etc.

It is important to this discussion to talk about oils. Fruits help to loosen and emulsify the sticky mucus wastes, partly by the oil in the skins. Lecithin and soft, raw, cold-pressed oils will also loosen and emulsify hardened oil (cholesterol) if the person has enough thyroid hormone ability to use the fats. Where this is not the case, fruit, nut, and vegetable oils, as naturally found in the whole fruit, are best. Fats are not as complex as proteins. There are essential fatty acids the body requires. The most readily used are the polyunsaturated, raw, uncooked, un-heated oils. These oils are found in fruit skins, nuts, vegetable seeds, or can be pressed from seeds, soybean, corn, the olive, etc. Starches and sugars begin their change in the mouth. Proteins are partly digested in the stomach. Carbohydrates continue digestion from the mouth to the stomach. As these processes are going on, fats are not affected much; but when they (the fats) arrive at the duodenum, bile from the gall bladder emulsifies fats and digestive enzymes from the pancreas gland attack carbohydrates, proteins, and fats; then on to the small intestine where elements are broken down further into simple sugars and are absorbed into the body.

189

It is my opinion that with these unsaturated or raw oils, as found in the above, and especially fruit, when the ascorbic acid is present, the process is much simpler. The ascorbic acid acts like a catalyst to spread the oil rapidly to the various parts with little change, causing an emul-sion even before reaching the duodenum where the gall bile can break it down much faster, similar to the way hand lotions or oils placed on the surface of the skin must have the acid to cause emulsion and allow the oil to penetrate the surface of the skin. It is my opinion that this takes place easily in the mouth when the oils are in combination with ascor-bic acid foods, such as fruit, etc., causing less work and energy used so the oil can quickly be dispersed to the various parts of the body for fuel and lubrication and that if cooked or heated, even oils from skins of fruits, nuts, etc., will have to be broken down by the gall bile when it reaches the duodenum, as oils harden in the process of heating.

You may wonder then why fruit or honey causes burning in the stomach during a fast in some cases if fruit diet is superior. Here again, we must go back to the hormone balance. It is like saying, "Which came first, the chicken or the egg?" Did the wrong diet cause imbalance in the internal secretions and hormones, or did the lack of hormone cause the problem? In some cases, I believe the weakness in glandular imbalance is hereditary; in others, it is caused by wrong combinations and constant abuse of the body. A severe traumatic experience can also cause glandular imbalance, like shock grief, etc. We may observe in this imbalance a lack of hydrochloric acid where the stomach is unable to digest foods. In these cases the hormone, if added to the diet in an herb form, helps to make digestion possible, also foods rich in Vitamin C and cleansing herbs will help. There is also a certain acid gas build-up which happens when high glucose and sugar foods begin to be mixed with stagnant toxic waste, causing a fermentation. It is in these cases that herbs are of such value, helping to neutralize the acids and reduce the gas. These are the bitter herbs we used to call the "bitters." It has been learned by some, in cases where toxic waste is very chronic, as in cancer, that pancreatin plays a part in the destruction or digestion of such waste, minimizing the problems of elimination. It is not necessary to use the animal pancreatin; the bitter herbs accomplish the same thing. It is necessary to use more vegetables at first, as has been explained; and as the body becomes cleaner, introduce fruits in abundance.

190　　　　There are both thin and fat type with Cushing's Pituitary Disease and Addison's Adrenal Disease or thyroid disease. There is the thin type that cannot put on weight and is not diabetic, where an excessive amount of the hormone is being secreted into the blood, such as thyroid where fat is used and burned too rapidly. Often, however, in the thin type, toxic waste is still stored in tissues and remains in the blood because of incorrect nutrition. There can be much chronic sickness in thin tissue which obstructs and causes damage to the various organs of the body. When a correct nutritional diet or a fast is used, the thin person responds much faster generally because the fat waste does not have to be eliminated. The thin person has difficulty staying on a cleansing diet because of the fear of losing weight. They will lose weight at first; but as the body heals, a normal weight will be reached. It has been my experience to see a man and wife, for example, both living on a mild food diet, where the overweight man lost weight, while his extremely thin wife gained. Her weight gain, prior to this, had been impossible using the most fattening foods. This brings us to the much-talked-about hypoglycemia.

Hypoglycemia is a malfunction of the adrenal glands. The adrenal cortex has two parts: the medulla, which secretes the hormone adrenalin, allowing us to fight or run in emergency; and the cortex, which secretes the hormone cortin. This hormone allows us to stand daily stress and worry. There are other hormones which have been found in the adrenal glands, but we will discuss only these two.

It is believed by some that when an abundance of blood sugar is placed in the cell and is not used as energy (use of muscle, etc.), it breaks down sugar into pyruvate, then pyruvate changes to heat, water, and carbon dioxide. When too much sugar is in the cell for normal activity, then pyruvate's end product is lactic acid.This same lactic acid build-up occurs from abnormal amounts of exercise, causing soreness of muscles. The usual process is for the lactic acid to return to the liver and be changed to glycogen and used again as energy. But in cases of hypoglycemia or adrenal cortical malfunction, sometimes during this recycling process some lactic acid remains and is returned to the cells, resulting in a build-up of lactic acid in the cells. Since lactic acid has an attraction to sodium and calcium, calcium builds up in the soft tissues; causing a deficiency for use by the body. Also, sodium is retained in the body, causing a deficiency of sodium for use, and the fluid builds. This build-up of fluid, especially in abdominal areas, interferes with transfer of nutrients through the intestinal membrane, causing a deficiency of all nutrients. The nerve fiber responds to large amounts of sodium in the cell, sending a message through the fiber saying, "inflow of sodium in cell" so cells become more and more ready to fire, causing a spontaneous firing (muscle twitching, grabbing, even epileptic seizures, a series of muscle firing over and over). This accounts for the burning sensations over the entire body at times experienced by the hypoglycemic. (I believe this happens also in the fat-type diabetes before wasting begins.) It is at this point, as muscle fibers begin to contract and pull tight across the joint, that a calcium build-up occurs. The body will sometimes place calcium on the pressured joints to protect the joint from damage. My thinking is in complete agreement with this theory, and I also believe that in the case of the thin type where the adrenal gland is not functioning calcium, magnesium, sodium, potassium, and phosphorus are spilled off into the urine (no tests have been made) or is at least not as the foregoing build-up in the cell due to lactic acid, because the thin type does not seem to have the acid-burning sensations or the digestive problems noted in the fat type, with the exception of where wrong combinations of food are eaten. The fluid build-up in the stomach retards digestion, sometimes bringing it to a complete stop. It is my opinion that if Vitamin B complex, B6, calcium, and potassium are used, the lactic acid flow will normalize to its natural route through the liver; fluid will move out, and the burning sensations will stop, with, of course, the addition of the necessary herbs.

Where we have the acid build-up, the colon is affected, causing the smooth muscles to become sluggish. Under stress and a lack of hormone, potassium is spilled off. The lack of potassium causes muscle weakness, as somehow potassium is not utilized in lactic acid build-up. It is potassium which gives tone to the muscles. Weakness and fatigue which bring on depression are, in my opinion, the result of this weakening of muscle tone. The heart, being a muscle, is also affected; and also, as some believe calcium to be a tranquilizer to most of the muscle mass of the body, causes the heart to become agitated by the lack of calcium which is bound up and held in the cells by lactic acid. Then the lactic acid which can be used by the heart muscle mass as fuel brings on palpitations, causing the heart to act like a car getting too much fuel.

Most people who are hypoglycemic are their own worst enemy. They are usually people who place themselves on a high stress level and do not know how to do otherwise. They are worriers, perfectionists, and when they, by stress, bring themselves into a state of depression, immediately feel sorry for themselves and have a difficult time trying to figure a way out of the stress which caused the problem. First of all, they must learn to turn things off.When there is something that can be done about a problem, it should be taken care of immediately so as not to have it hanging in the back of the mind, stirring up troubles. Where there is nothing that can be done at the moment, forget it, turn it off, until such time as something can be done. They must overcome worry by adding faith to their lives, overcoming fear, learning to live in a peaceful aura. They must overcome self-pity and, of course, correct their diets, adding the herbs necessary to bring about a healthful condition.

In hypoglycemia where sugar is taken to give a stimulating lift in the hope of overcoming depression, the problem is compounded, as sugar leaches the Vitamin B and the calcium, causing more stress, losing more potassium and body tone. The insulin is raised to an unnatural high to take care of the sugar, somehow extending past its needs and afterwards dropping to a new low, causing a low blood sugar called insulin shock (overdose of insulin). Immediately we add sugar to lift us up again and a vicious circle has begun. Having found the herbs that act like cortisone (cortin hormone) to be helpful in this case, I feel it is important for me to make it known. To begin with, a brief history about cortisone may be of interest.

With the help of the African Witch Doctor, the seeds of the plant strophanthus were used to make cortisone or Compound E. Because of the rain forests and difficulty to harvest this plant, cortisone was later made from the Mexican wild yam. Also, because as has been said, either man feels he is smarter than God, or he wants to make more money, cortisone was made synthetically. When the adrenal glands begin to break down from too much stress (sometimes a shock, too much worry, or too much sugar eaten) we develop hypoglycemia or Addison's Disease. Addison's Disease is characterized by symptoms similar to hypoglycemia, as has been noted, with the addition that in Addison's Disease it has become terminal. According to medical standards, blotchy pigment appears suddenly on large parts of the body, intolerance to heat or cold, reduction in capacity for muscular work, weakness, inability to stand any stress or emotional excitement, negative or positive, sometimes nervous breakdown or even insanity, complete exhaustion, feeling you are going to die, inability to digest food, as has been discussed. When the cortin hormone is completely unproduced, the body dies as with lack of insulin. You can see by what has been said that the lack of cortin can also result, prior to Addison's Disease, in arthritis. The giving of cortisone for arthritis is a help only when adrenal malfunction is the cause. Where the cause is years of incorrect eating, it is worthless; but doctors continue to give it for anything and everything, in the hope they may find something else for which to use the new wonder drug. They have discovered that it helps in some skin disease; but here again, the skin problem was related to the stress factor involving the adrenals. Had they used a natural herb cortisone, they could have saved themselves the complications, side effects, and disillusionment that came from using the synthetic drug.

The herbs I know of that act as cortisone are licorice root and wild yam, licorice being the better. Licorice acts like a steroid. Cortisone is a steroid sugar. Licorice does not, however, bring the high insulin reaction that the sugar does. For a while, the hypoglycemic must remain on the ups and downs he has become used to until he, with herbs, can regulate the insulin-type herbs to the cortizone-type herbs. To clarify this, let me say that I believe it is the taking of sugar (sucrose) which brings on the shock associated with low blood sugar; adding a little goldenseal when taking too much sugar assists the body in its use. Goldenseal acts somewhat like insulin but does not increase the insulin to a shock rate, but rather somehow assists the body in the use of the sugar. Then to add something comparable to cortin (adrenal hormone), licorice can be used (as a steroid); licorice gives a better lift than sugar, without increasing the blood sugar demand for insulin and bringing on the shock. As I see it, the greatest enemy to the hypoglycemic person is sugar, but not the natural fruit sugars their bodies so desperately need.

All hormone herbs must be taken in different proportions by each person, according to his need, so it is impossible for me to say how much. Here again, we must learn to listen to the spirit. Perhaps if I told you how I came by the knowledge of hormone herbs you would understand what I mean.

Having studied diet and health, teaching exercise, even having had my own gym for women, along with fasting often, raising organic gardens, and knowing the results, I felt I had an edge on all truth, until I had a shocking, traumatic, painful grief that I just could not surmount. Within one year and a half, I had developed Addison's Disease. Knowing what I knew about the body and knowing what I knew about cortisone, that the life expectancy is only about ten years of taking this drug, I prayed to find a way to save my life. I knew I must take cortisone or die but felt there must be an herb which would act in this way. I had a blessing and was blessed that I would find the answer to my problem. Three days later, I found it — licorice. As I began to experiment with it, I found that if I took two 00-size capsules a day of powdered licorice root, I could go twenty-four hours. As soon as twenty-four hours were up, I would go back to feeling the same way. You may say, "Well, then, it must be addictive." So is eating; like insulin, it must be replaced when it is used up. I learned as my body healed, however, that when living on fruit only, licorice was not necessary. At first, the problems attached to adrenal malfunction would not allow fruit diets nor fasting. The vitamins and herbs necessary to restore, so as to be able to use more fruits are listed in the chapters on herbs and home remedies. You can stop taking licorice without going into shock as you would if you suddenly stopped taking cortisone. The spirit whispers many things; we must learn to listen. Gibby said,

"If you 'follow the herd' you'll soon be lost in the oblivion of thundering hoofs."

When people who have been under severe stress, overworking the adrenals and becoming extremely nervous and irritable, begin to take licorice, they think they have suddenly, spiritually, arrived. It is my opinion that many who suffer in mental institutions could be helped with this wonderful herb.

The use of estrogen has become quite popular after certain surgeries, but not without the side effects that seem to accompany the taking of drugs. The natural estrogen-type herb is black cohosh; there are many others which have a certain amount of estrogen, and I am sure there are many undiscovered. When black cohosh is used during menstrual cramps, the cramps stop within a few minutes. If ginger is added as a catalyst, the pain subsides much faster. Where nervousness is attributed to the lack of estrogen, black cohosh also works beautifully. Here again, you must play it by ear to decide amounts. When too much is taken, it causes a headache, otherwise no side effects, only the good effects of relaxation for the woman with the inability to produce estrogen who is ready to "climb the walls." Hormone herbs can be used together when more than one gland is affected. Black cohosh should not be used during pregnancy; often licorice or other hormone herbs are needed at that time, however.

The male hormone in herb form would be ginseng or sarsaparilla. Where a man has prostate gland problems, the usual cause is impactions of waste matter in the lower bowel, filled with worms. The swelling will usually go down after eating pumpkin seeds to kill the worms. Other things to assist will be listed in the section on home remedies. It should be mentioned here, however, that men go through a deterioration process as do women while the ageing is taking place, along with a reduction in the production of necessary hormones. So assistance with the natural herb male hormone is of great benefit.

Another gland which causes a great deal of difficulty is the pituitary. The disease related to the lack of pituitary hormone has often to do with growth, as in dwarf or giant; but as the body reaches maturity, sometimes the incorrect production of this hormone causes the disease we call Cushing's Disease to develop. Its symptoms are similar to Addison's Disease, as are its causes, the one marked difference being the rapid deterioration of the female productive organs, similar to what happens during the change of life. In most cases, the fat type will be the result, with fast, excessive weight gain, problems with the menstrual period (scanty or irregular), the inability to carry a baby to full term, and extreme nervousness and fatigue. The pituitary hormone is alfalfa. To solve the problem, it has been taken in as high a dose as twenty tablets a day, and licorice and sometimes black cohosh are also necessary to bring about a desired result.

195

The overweight condition, where it exists in Addison's and Cushing's diseases, will not in all cases entirely be solved by the taking of hormone-type herbs. In most cases, when using a mild food diet, the weight will come down, but in some cases it will not. It has been my experience that when taking any concentrated foods, the herbs, somehow acting as if the body had produced the hormone, use it to assist in the use of these foods. It has also been my experience with Addison's and Cushing's diseases, in the fat type, that certain minerals and vitamins must be added before much fruit can be tolerated. However, as the body cleans and changes, the fruit becomes the most perfect diet for these types if weight loss is desired, as sometimes only then will the weight come down. It has also been observed that no hormone-type herbs need to be taken when living solely on a fruit and nut diet. It is as if the body is in need of the hormone only to aid with the use of the foods which must make more of a change. The weight will usually normalize in diabetics or thyroid-caused hormone imbalance with the use of mild food and the necessary hormone. Sometimes the body will go back to a normal condition, and no more hormone herbs are needed no matter what the diet. Other times, the body is just not able to produce enough hormone to live a normal life without help. That it is possible with these herbs to restore the glands to where they will again produce, I have seen. That they will always produce on their own, I cannot say, as sometimes, either by birth or because of irrepairable damage, the glands will never produce and they will have to continue on herbs for life. Then, of course, as I have suggested, some people keep themselves on a high stress level and will always need more than they can produce. It is interesting to note that the ancient Greek and Roman armies gave their soldiers licorice, and they carried it on their persons as our boys have carried penicillin. It was given to allay thirst, but it may have done another thing of which they were not aware. It could have been the reason they were able to stand the terrible stress of war from childhood until maturity and still be the strongest, healthiest, continual armies the world has known. Certainly we in our day live under stress, but war is not a way of life with us as with the Romans. Our stress is certainly comparable, however, and I do not feel it is going to get any better. People may come to learn that a little licorice when under stress is superior to a sedative or a pain killer for the resultant headache that sometimes follows heavy stress.

The thyroid gland often has a related attachment to any of the other glands' malfunctioning, but sometimes its problems are singular. It has been noted that the thyroid gland seems to be low in iodine when the body is undergoing a toxic contagion, a cold, etc. It has been noted to be low also in chronic disease. It has been noted by the swelling of the throat, as in goiter, that the gland is more active at this time, and the iodine content is lower. It has been taught that when iodine is taken by mouth, a considerable portion is taken up by the thyroid; likewise, when iodine is set free in the blood by the thyroid hormone, the thyroid promptly takes back most of the iodine, sort of a recycling process. It has been taught that the body practices great economy with respect to iodine, utilizing the bulk of its store over and over in the hormone synthesis of iodine derived from the daily breakdown, and that only a fraction is excreted; 0.2 milligrams of iodine per day is required to make thyroid hormone. The average adult intake, using an ordinary diet, is 0.03 milligrams; seven times this amount is required for hormone production. Keeping this in mind, it would indicate to me that swelling or infection caused by toxic waste increases the need for iodine, also increasing the amount being sent out into circulation to kill the bacteria.If it were used up, rendering it unable to recycle, it would show up on the B.M.R. (basic metabolic rate) as being lowered.

Other hormones, as it has been shown, are used up — why not iodine? When there is not enough iodine to perform its functions and too much waste is added to the body, the thyroid works in a way we could call active, struggling like whipping a tired horse, into the swelling condition we call goiter. The thing that interests me is that you can use kelp or dulse for what is termed hypo- or hyper-thyroid, inactive or overactive, with the result that the gland improves. This is not the case with the thyroid drug.

When there is a lack of iodine, such as would whip the tired horse even further, a state we call cretin or myxedema results. The cretin or myxedema condition further proves my theory by their being unable to combat acute disease. They always have a cold, constipation, respiratory problems, etc. They also die at a very young age in cretinism, and soon in case of myxedema, if something is not done. It is well known that an inadequate hormone production of the thyroid causes cretin condition during fetal or early life and a myxedema condition at any time in life, but it is not known why. Out of the same causes we have discussed, too much mucus waste in the body, the glands of thyroid and neck can harden, developing a cement-like mucus in the entire area causing, also, the related ear trouble. By the glands swelling, they can force the vertebrae of the neck to move over, pinching nerves, thus causing other problems. The bowel can be affected and the heart also. If this mucus remains too long, it can become tumorous or cancerous. Myxedema can also result where there has been a removal of the thyroid, developing very rapidly the person taking on the appearance of the cretin. Severe myxedema may cause wasting rather than obesity, a state of cachexia as in malignancies.

There are two tests to determine the activity of the thyroid: B.M.R. (basal metabolic rate) and P-B-I (protein bound iodine). In the case of hypo- (under) active, the symptoms are goiter, cretinism, myxedema, and obesity. The B.M.R. would show normal or low, while the P-B-I would be low. The treatment used in the medical world would be iodine. The symptoms with hyper- (over) active would be high pulse, hypertension, protrusion of the eyeballs, atrial fibrillation, overactive heart, sometimes enlarged. Older persons may be apathetic, with heart failure. Wasting can also occur, and the P-B-I would show high, the medical treatment usually being surgical removal of part of the gland to reduce its

197

activity or any tumor. A new treatment is the use of radioactive iodine, with the theory being that if the gland is producing too much iodine, radioactive iodine will pick it up, possibly destroying part of the gland. What then happens to all that radioactivity?

It is considered that the thyroid's actions in the body are metabolism of protein and carbohydrates, fat, water, and salt; growth, nervous, muscular, and circulatory; and endocrine glands. Some people are given the thyroid drug to lose weight in an attempt to swing their bodies over from underactive to overactive so as to burn off the fat. Some people are given radioactive iodine to stop the over-production. As I have said, when the kelp or dulse iodine works well in either case, I cannot help but believe they are completely off the track when it comes to treatment of the thyroid. The medical manuals and books on the thyroid seem to be a mass of confused contradictions.

It is my opinion that the thyroid becomes weakened and its function is either over-or under-active because of too much mucus waste, where it either gives up or is over-stimulated, the way a hypoglycemic goes into insulin shock by over-production. When the body keeps increasing the toxic body waste, calling for more iodine, the thyroid can swing either way, as I see it, depending on its ability to produce hormone.

198

Just because only a small amount of iodine is excreted does not necessarily mean that iodine is recycled as it is used; it could be used up, finished. Where there is an over-production caused by the necessity to combat bacteria (too much mucus), the over-production could have an effect like that of taking iodine poison. Where the correct amount is sent forth into the body, it could have the positive effect of killing germs like painting iodine on a wound. It is my opinion also that the tonsil secretes iodine, killing the bacteria as it enters the mouth; and when we remove the tonsil, we remove its helpful insurance against invading bacteria.

When the body is clean and cleared of toxic waste, the glands' function becomes normal. You can even put a cretin or mongoloid child on the herb iodine and a mild food diet, and they remain free from their usual constipation and constant colds. In these cases I feel it would be possible to bring the child back to normal, provided no brain damage were part of the problem. Perhaps I have not come to the correct reasons why, but I do know that mild food and herbs can change the problems with the glands. It has been my personal observation that the adding of iodine kelp or dulse in acute disease assists just like the painting of iodine on a sore throat. However, it should not be takeen at the same time as Vitamin C, as they destroy one another. At any rate, I feel that medical science is looking in the wrong direction for its answers related to the thyroid gland, making a fairly simple thing into a very complex problem.

Dr. N. W. Walker has done some excellent work on raw juice formulas for the glands and lists the following mineral requirements. I recommend his books *Become Younger* and *Raw Vegetable Juices.*In addition, I am adding the vitamins most necessary. A multiple vitamin should be used in all cases. Listed are the specific vitamins and minerals most necessary for individual glands.

PITUITARY (Cushing's Disease, dwarf or giant)

Min. & Vit. Needed:	Drug Used:	Herbs that have been used:
Phosphorus	ATCH	Alfalfa
Sulphur		
Manganese		
Iodine		
Vitamin B		

(Where insipidus diabetes, caused by the pituitary, is present alfalfa should be used along with insulin-type herbs. Pitressin extract of animal pituitary has been the medical treatment.)

PANCREAS (Diabetes, Cancer)

Min. & Vit. Needed:	Drug Used:	Herbs that have been used:
Chlorine	Insulin	Goldenseal
Magnesium		Juniper berries
Potassium		
Sodium		
Calcium		
Vitamin B		

LIVER (Acidosis, Raised pressure)

Min. & Vit. Needed:	Drug used:	Herbs that have been used:
Sodium		Lemon
Chlorine		Goldenseal
Potassium		
Magnesium		
Vitamin C		

LYMPH GLANDS (Toxemia)

Min. & Vit. Needed:	Drug Used:	Herbs that have been used:
Calcium		CS formula
Fluorine		
Iron		
Silicon		
Vitamin C		

THYMUS (Degeneration)

Min. & Vit. Needed:
Calcium
Fluorine
Iron
Silicon
Multiple Vitamin

ADRENALS (Hypoglycemia, Addison's Disease)

Min. & Vit. Needed:		**Drug Used:**	**Herbs that have been used:**
(Part one	(Part two	Cortisone	Licorice or wild yam
Cortex)	Medulla)		
Calcium	Phosphorus		
Fluorine	Sulphur		
Iron	Iodine		
Silicon	Manganese		
B Complex	Vitamin B		
With edema			
Potassium			
B6 where colon is ulcerated			

PINEAL — Considered by Eastern religions to be the spiritual gland

Min. & Vit. Needed:	**Herbs that have been used:**
Iodine	Pineal formula
Manganese	
Phosphorus	
Sulphur	

THYROID (Goiters, cretin, hypo or hyper)

Min. & Vit. Needed:	**Drug Used:**	**Herbs that have been used:**
Iodine	Thoraxine	Dulse
Chlorine	Iodine	Kelp
Magnesium	Radioactive	
Potassium	Iodine	
Sodium		

PARA THYROID (Fat over Abdomen and hips)

Min. & Vit. Needed:	**Herbs that have been used:**
Potassium	Dulse or kelp
Magnesium	
Iodine	
Chlorine	
Sodium	

SPLEEN (High blood pressure and premature old age)

Min. & Vit. Needed:
Chlorine
Magnesium
Potassium
Sodium

Herbs that have been used:
Dulse or kelp

MAMMARY GLANDS (Cancer, tumors)

Min. & Vit. Needed:
Calcium
Fluorine
Iron
Silicon

Herbs that have been used:
CS or CT formula

OVARIES (Cancer, tumors)

Min. & Vit. Needed:
Calcium
Fluorine
Iron
Silicon

Herbs that have been used:
CS or CT formula

PROSTATE (Impotency, cancer, tumors)

Min. & Vit. Needed:
Calcium
Fluorine
Iron
Silicon

Herbs that have been used:
CS or CT formula
Prostate formula
Pumpkin seeds

There has been little really known regarding acid alkaline body balance. It has been taught that there is danger in being too alkaline. This danger exists only when meat and starch are eaten in large quantities. When the body is unable to develop the necessary acids, hydrochloric, etc. to use meats and starches, the disease is considered terminal and the alkalinity is blamed. It is not recognized that the body in its effort to heal the gland is trying to alkalize. When alkalinity tests are done showing an alkaline body the person is told to eat more meat, because an alkaline condition is dangerous. In order for the body to use acid forming concentrated foods, an acid is a necessary part of digestion such as hycrochloric acid, enzymes, etc., produced by the glands. Where the glands are out of balance, heavy protein and starch cannot be tolerated. If a person lives for an extended period of time on a mild food, or alkaline diet, it is with difficulty that they can jump back and forth to acid forming concentrated foods. There should be a gradual change and demand on the glands.

Where glands are in a weak condition and where the person is under heavy stress, an attempt to jump too quickly back to a lot of meat, starch or sugar will cause acid burning, as nature overshoots her mark in order to handle the newly introduced concentrated foods, much like the hypoglycemic brings on an insulin shock from heavy intake of sugar. This burning is much more intense than heartburn and can burn holes in the stomach and intestines. This is much of the cause of colitis in the hypoglycemic or an Addison disease type. When the body is in this heavy acid burning state, sugar should not be eaten, not even glucose fruit sugar (honey or fruit), as it sets up a fermentation that causes the acid to increase to unbearable heights. Even gold and silver rings will turn green on the hands. A quick alkalinity is necessary to bring it down. To relieve the burning, high vitamin C, as with a cold, vegetable diet, slippery elm or okra may be used. Calcium, potassium, magnesium and vitamin B complex are helpful. Check food charts where vitamins are not available to find foods which are high in these elements. Lots of water always helps to put out the fire.

There is nothing wrong with an alkaline body; it is the most perfectly well and clean. After a cold or a cleanse of the body, it will always show alkaline. As we begin to introduce meat, starch, and sugar after a cold, we sometimes feel sick at the stomach.

202   Where the glands are out of balance and the case has gone so far as not to be able to use meats, starches, and sugar, the herbs acting in a similar way to cortizone, ATCH, insulin, etc., usually allow the person to handle these foods. Where damage is too extensive, the person must remain on a vegetable and fruit diet to live. Where vegetables are eaten in this case the hormone herbs must be used. When only fruit and nuts are used, the herbs are not necessary. Sometimes, on such a diet the glands will restore, and if a normal diet is desired, a gradual change back to concentrated foods is required.

Eating more starch to soak up the acid does not solve the problem. Sooner or later the person will take an anti-acid, soda pop or liquor, thus compounding the problem. Some people live every day of their lives with an anti-acid. What a waste. It is only in the alkaline body that healing takes place. It is only in the alkaline body that the body will release its toxic waste in a healing crisis or cleanse, except where it reaches its height of toxicity and nature forces an acute condition (a disease crisis as has been mentioned before). Do not be afraid of being over alkaline. If we have not the character to resist the meats, starches and sugars as we try to clean our bodies, use a little apple cider vinegar or some of the bitter herbs with meals and the over action of acid that happens when glands are not functioning can be avoided. You may not be aware of it, but this is the reason so many people drink hard liquor to assist the disfunctioning glands to digest concentrated foods. This, of course, is an insane remedy, to whip an already exhausted glandular system by adding the life destroying elements of liquor; some people do the same things with drugs. An over-acid condition also often results when eating too much starch, meat, sugar, or using wrong combinations of foods and becomes a cause of pimples, acid stomach, indigestion, skin rash, boils and canker sores. With insufficient insulin the diabetic can go into an acid condition which can bring on coma. Antacids, insulin and glucose are used to bring the condition to normal. The herb insulin can prevent this, along with a mild food diet.

The herb insulin also has the healing effect of preventing the hemorrhages as it can stop internal bleeding. The vitreous part of the eye will often hemorrhage in diabetes causing the retina to pull away from the choroid or feeding organ and thus deteriorating from lack of contact with its food source. Use of the natural herb can prevent this from happening.

Natural herb type insulin is very healing to the open wound, ulceration or burn, but for too long we have tried to clear the skin with expensive preparations when all healing really takes place first from the inside.

It would not be right to teach about health without calling to your attention the importance of exercise. There are people who believe exercise is the living end to all truth until certain body parts begin to wear out to the extent that vigorous exercise can no longer be accomplished. There have been some very interesting experiments made before sending man into outer space. Knowing as we do that atrophy sets in when muscles are unused, and that muscles would be unused for an extended period of time as in space, they realized this problem had to be overcome. They learned that weights could not be used in a weightless condition, so isometric and isotonic exercises were used. After having been a real physical fitness nut, and having lifted weights for twenty years or so, I had to learn the hard way that extreme measures in exercise are not all that necessary. When you are in the position, as has been explained, where exercise increases lactic acid and causes a constant burning, you will try to get along without exercise. I have since learned that the replacing of calcium, certain of the B complex, and potassium supplements stops or slows down the lactic acid build-up so the body can again be exercised. Therefore, I have come to believe that vigorous exercise at certain times is not for everyone. The interesting thing about exercise is that it can be much overdone both in work and in play. Statistics show the heavy laborer's life span is shorter than that of the rich playboy who exercises for fun. We only need to do sufficient exercise so as to be able to call on a reserve in case of emergency. There have recently been some wonder programs put forth for the retarded which would be well worth looking into. These methods are suffering a travail of birth as they, like Sister Kenny, attempt to get past the powers that be. It has been found that a child cannot learn in a normal manner often when the foundation of so simple a thing as crawling has been by-passed. These new methods give hope to those who have had brain damage or are retarded in one way or another. Exercise is an important part of our existence. As in all phases of our lives, atrophy sets in rapidly when we are inactive. Gibby said,

"Life is like swimming, you must keep moving to stay on top."

There have been many things discussed which may, when used, help you to better understanding, sufficient to help yourself to a healthier way of life; but I could not conclude without telling you what I have learned about the care of the colon. The large intestine is the cesspool of the body. The small intestine is essential in the absorption of nutrients into the body. When either becomes clogged, self-poisoning is the result. The large intestine is not as absorptive, as it is made of tougher material. It does absorb, however, so when waste remains too long, hardening and rotting poisons are absorbed into the blood.

204

A young doctor, writing for a newspaper, made the statement in answer to an old man's question about constipation, that seems to be typical of medical science's understanding of how the body feeds and eliminates. He said that as you grow older, it is not necessary to have a bowel movement every day, and it did not matter if you did not for four or five days. He further said you should not take laxatives. If it could only be known that most of the ills of mankind begin in the intestinal tract. When you begin to look into each other's eyes, you will see as I have, the truth of this statement. How is the waste from all over the body going to eliminate if the bowel is blocked? Yes, a strain will then be placed on the kidneys and other avenues of elimination. Many of the problems people have with the skin can be traced to the bowel, with the kidneys not being able to handle added burden, and out it pops on the skin, always in an effort to keep you alive.

The small intestines are your life-line to food nutrients; when they are clogged with tumors, parasites, and the hardened oil of cholesterol lining their walls, you cannot expect to be properly fed. To take a laxative would certainly be better, it seems to me, than to remain clogged. We smile at the laxative commercials on TV, but who of us has not recognized the dizzy headache and stuffy, tired feeling that accompanies constipation. It has been my observation that where certain sections of the colon are clogged or impacted, certain diseases or malfunction of other parts of the body relate; for example, when there are impactions in the rectum, the uterus and prostate are affected. Where impactions are present at the lower descending colon, the bladder is affected. The center of the descending colon affects the kidneys and adrenals, close to the splenic flexure, the pancreas. Certain places on the traverse colon affect the stomach, throat, bronchials, esophagus, trachea, gall bladder, and heart. Just below the hepatic flexure, impactions affect the liver; and the ascending colon clogged can cause hayfever, asthma, vitamin deficiency, bad tonsils, nasal mucus, sinus, and has an effect on the pituitary gland. The appendix is actually the overflow valve or safety factor to keep impacted waste matter from pushing back into the small intestines where the poisons would be absorbed into the blood. This is why people who have had their appendix removed often get dizzy or nauseated while taking an enema. Whenever nausea or dizziness occurs during an enema or colonic irrigation, it should be stopped immediately until softened waste matter can remove from the ascending colon. The argument against taking an enema will often be, "I don't have any problems like that; I have a normal bowel movement every day." This is possible, and it is still possible to have an impaction in one area or another while experiencing a daily movement. The large intestine is like a balloon: if it is squeezed down in one place, it balloons out in another, and vice versa.

205

16)

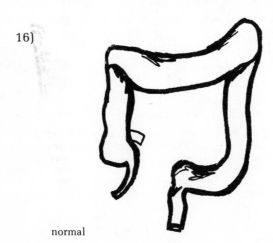

normal

17)

18)

Some places could have a very small passageway leaving other places impacted for

years and years of uneliminated waste, continually poisoning the body.

206

19)   20)   21)

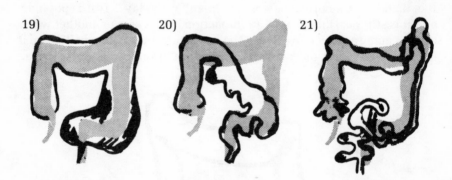

When the colon balloons out at the lower part of the decending colon, it has to automatically squeeze down to small at the anus, causing hemorrhoids, fissures, tearing, and bleeding ulcers in the rectum where hardened waste stays and rots. The colon can become distorted into all kinds of shapes and can pinch together and adhere to itself, causing scar tissue and becoming small in places.

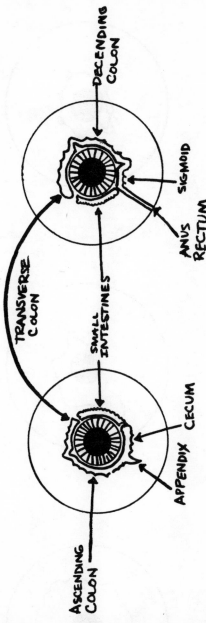

When the colon becomes ulcerated because of what I have shown you, nature tries to force the wastes out by causing a diarrhea. Medical doctors will tell you one of the first symptoms of colitis or cancer of the colon is a continual diarrhea condition. It is very interesting that you can see by the iris of the eye exactly where the colon is impacted. You can determine whether it is prolapsed, normal, or distended, for example:

23)

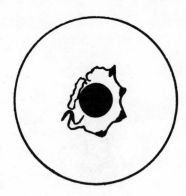

208

24)

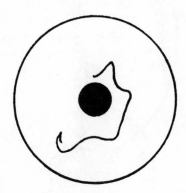

25)

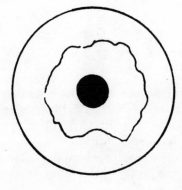

When you watch the magic that happens to the colon line on the eyes and feel the magic that happens as health is improved, when the colon is cleared and cleaned, you could not possibly believe that constipation has nothing to do with health.

Even the enemas given in the hospitals are a disgrace, causing the constipation you have noticed after an operation or having a baby. They pump two quarts of water into the lower descending colon and tell you to hold it no matter what impactions may be in the descending colon, thus distending the lower bowel. What happens to a balloon when you blow it up? Yes, it loses its elasticity, and that is exactly what happens when the lower colon is distended by two quarts of water. Then as the waste matter from above moves down, it fills up the larger distended area, closing smaller at the anus, rather than being moved out; matter will then usually stay and harden and we then have constipation.

My idea of the correct way to take an enema is to first of all lie on the left side. Make sure the hose is free of air bubbles by allowing it to run some water through first. Insert tip, allowing warm water to run in until the least cramp is felt, then expel. Keep doing this continually, introducing water and expelling it even if you have to do it over and over many times, a little at a time, until water reaches the waistline, never taking any more water than will cause a cramp. When water can be felt at the waistline, turn on the back, continuing in the same way, cleaning the transverse colon. When water has reached the waist at the right side, turn over onto the right side and clean the ascending side. By the time the entire colon has been cleaned in this way, usually taking in the process two bags full, a little at a time, the third bag will usually go the entire length of the colon and the water expelled will be clear. Warm water at first relaxes and causes less cramping. Cool water tones like astringent and is best in the last water taken.

There is in use in some hospitals, a drug solution in a small amount which effects an evacuation. This amount of fluid to give an enema does not distend the lower bowel as much, but what does the drug do to the bowel?

Herbs helpful to the colon are listed in the section on home remedies.

CHAPTER EIGHT

CONCLUSION

Where can we go to find a physician of intellectual integrity coupled with aesthetic refinement, who sends out sparks of energy in all directions? Where is there such a man to bear our personal solitary burden? Where is there such a man filled with the mood of philanthropy, who would not charge us beyond our ability to pay? Where is there a man whose benevolent and idealistic mind cannot be corrupted by money? Where is this selfless man who radiantly performs miracles? What have we done that we crown the physician to be God over us reinforcing his fragile being with the props of our own imaginations? Have we lowered ourselves to the relinquishment of our own responsibility to ourselves and to our God by trusting in the arm of flesh? As my words ring out strong and defiant against the powers that be in the medical world of today, it is not with the hope that I might render all medical practice null and void. We cannot be cut off from all comforting sustaining contact with our fellowmen, nor can we be cut off from the medicines God has given to be used for those who lack the faith to be healed.

Certainly there are many in the field of natural medicine also who are filled with corruption and greed; therefore, understand I do not condone all they do either. There are some claiming natural methods who swing a pendulum, rejecting the providential procedures of the gift of the spirit while they accept the illusions of satanic forces until by their acts of faith in him they bring Satan into their lives and the lives of their patients, and by miracles they bring conviction. Satan does not always tell the truth, though he may often perform that we may believe. There are even some who assume that evil can tell no truth while they themselves, believing so, have become subject to Satan's kingdom for they have not read the scripture that tells of his appearance as an angel of light. There are also those in the natural health field who, for a price of

$50 or so, send out prayers touched with electricity and certain herbal remedies, curing people miles away. Since when has God dealt in prayer money? After a long illness or a terminal death sentence, people can become easy prey to all the evils interwoven into the many methods of the so-called art of healing.

Have I made it all seem hopelessly complex? Do you want to believe the programs and procedures I have put forth? Until we learn to live by the spirit in righteousness, there is nothing we can know for sure, and where life is at stake, one compliance with the wrong concept can be a disastrous and suicidal decision. For many, these decisions have already been made to their destruction, as they allow men to give them drugs or needless surgery or as they patronize the men with the pendulum or the offer to pray for them for money.

You may say, "How can I know if I am living in the spirit? How can I be free of reservation? Why do I still harbor doubts?" To know all things would be to be a god. To have light given a little at a time is the way we grow from childhood. This is the easy and peaceful way, the way of trust and hope without fear.

211

> "Except ye become as a little child ye cannot enter the kingdom of God."

To walk always in trust, knowing all things are done for our benefit, growth, and development, is to become as a little child.

> "Search diligently, pray always and be believing and all things shall work together for your good, if you walk uprightly."

We often lose track of this goal by walking stubbornly our own way, regardless of the spirit of Christ that whispers to us how wrong we are. In the occult religions prevalent among some of the young people of today, an evil philosophy is spreading like wildfire, sweeping away childlike faith with its insidious teaching that you can by concentration cause anything to happen in your favor and by the witness that if it is favorable to you, you can be sure it is of God. It is like saying, "If I can concentrate enough, I could cause a lamp to turn on without knowing anything about its source or its laws." When anything happens to us by prayer in the way of a miracle where we know nothing about the laws relative to the reward, it can come from only two sources, either from God or from Satan, never is it because of our own ability. Satan knows also the laws of the universe and uses them to cause a miracle, like moving a table or giving you answers. He uses also the principle of faith, or concentrated meditation, and gives the rewards of proof, one of his many tactics. How can we then know if a miracle was caused by our own valiant compliance to the rules or by the result of the adversary? The tendency to sacrifice and a fanatical pursuit of exactitude is often the likely consequence from either position, where sometimes the person who thinks he is moving the table must also live an aesthetic life of sacrifice, with a kindly, benevolent attitude. How can we know where to place our faith?

When we are able to live any law, all the struggle goes out of it; and we become free of the torment of trial and error. As long as any of the rules are broken, we are torn. God does not have to show forth his power to prove He is God. He does not move tables for the amazement of our friends, to justify our own self-righteousness and magnify it before others. It is enough that the sun rises each day to justify belief in God. When He does show forth his power, it is to cleanse the wicked from the earth; in the meantime, he patiently waits on all of us. That faith is rewarded of God it is true, but Christ told those who had been healed to go their way and tell no man. To expect that God would move always by what we concentrated to bring into being would be to believe that we are smarter than He. No, He has set down His rules, and bits and pieces of them are spread through the wide expanse of all religious faith and all peoples who have ever lived upon the earth. When we go against the basic truths we know inside ourselves, the time-honored truths whispered to all of us by the spirit of Christ of correct morality, we walk in the paths of evil and the pride of our hearts.

When we walk with our hand in God's as a child, struggling to obey His rules, patiently accepting those things that happen to us as we strive for perfection, thankful for what we receive, asking for what we want, and, as a child, waiting on the Lord, knowing that in His good time He will give us always that which is for our benefit — then will the real miracles fill our lives with the joy of confident security. When we learn the true principles of obedience to certain laws, we can tap into that great store as the light of truth filters down through us to bless mankind with the creativity of great music, art, literature, or wisdom, then we become an open vessel, an instrument of God to bless us and mankind. This is the great miracle of faith, not done for our own aggrandizement, but rather to bless us, the world, and our fellowmen.

Herein lies the difference, a positive attitude that all things are working for our best good, not a positive attitude so as to have everything we want. By the principle of faith we can bring to ourselves good or evil. We can have anything we want if we want it badly enough, and it can be a blessing or a pain to us. The secret lies in being careful what it is that we demand.

Faith is not an apathetic resignation, seeking serenity no matter what suffering nor how pitfully low we may descend, enduring all defeats with submissive acceptance; but rather it is a working, striving, goal-setting, going concern with a positive belief in the ultimate good. When we have trials or setbacks, our reactions are neither bitter, nor are they failure complexes. Faith is the joy of peaceful, cheerful living, knowing in the process of failure we can learn, ever fashioning in our lives the beauty of perfected precision intimately linked with Deity.

Among some of the young people there are many counter-cultures spreading, with the Eastern ideals as their source, having a gradual undermining effect on our contemporary world. Some are positive; most are negative, because they lack the strengthening power of Christianity. One I should mention here, which if reinforced by Christianity, could do a great deal to help us to a healthier way of life. Talking with a young man steeped in modern hippie philosophies, I came away feeling sad that he could not, with the great intelligence I could see he possessed, discover what this life is really all about. He had learned to become very aware in the world of nature. He could see such beauty in nature and in natural foods. He said he could talk to the plants and they would move in response. When in the discussion I said, "I do not believe we were intended to live with plants out always in the open in the same way animals live. And man was placed here to subdue the earth." He then said he would rather be an animal. He said animals would not do the things men do to each other.

Where in the philosophy of Christianity and in the cultures developing in America today can we find mutual understanding? We as Christian city people need to go back to the land and learn to enjoy the beauty of nature, with the use of correct foods for nourishment or medicine. We certainly need to live the principle of brotherly love and morality in order to be an example to these youngsters. The way it is today, there is an acute conflict of personality, an almost chemically-negative reaction to one another, the generation gap. There needs to be more love on both sides. The young people involved in this new morality need to add to their new knowledge of nature the sound principles of cleanliness, time-proven morality, and true Christian brotherly love — so lacking in their philosophy. They will argue, "We are the only ones who love." Is it love to walk away from parents who have sacrificed their lives for them? Is it love or is it lust which lives without commitment? Is it love to have no responsibility to the world or to each other? Is it love to drop out of the race and let someone else do the work? Is it love to tear down all established rules, good or bad? Is it love to distrust everyone over thirty? Is it love to look upon the aged with contempt and scorn?

The thing that distinguishes man from the animal is the spirit of self-sacrificing love of others. This is the grandest and most noble attribute of man. This is the foundation of a happy marriage. Animals grub in the dirt, fight each other for their food, and only on the TV shows do they sacrifice themselves for another animal. Mother bird will fight or limp away to distract, but only by accident will she give her life for her babies. Only for the approval of man will an animal give of himself. Among the animals, living by instinct, it is the survival of the fittest. Man, on the other hand, lives as a reasoning being with Godlike attributes which should cause him to care for others. How much he does care determines his stature and his closeness to the fulfillment of his Godlike destiny. If the young people absorbed in such a strange ideology could walk the streets of some oriental countries and see the people, like animals defecating on the streets and then walking barefooted in it, they may not be so ready to bring our civilization back to grubbing in the dirt. They may see that the sudden rush of events has swept them off their feet into a corrupting and strange environment which removes them far from harmony with God's plan for his children.

When we sit back looking through the "glass, darkly," scoffing at the weakness of religious people and church, using the word "hypocrite" to justify our own lack of faith, we can never quite open our vessel wide enough to receive the manifestations of the spirit which the Lord reserves for those who have faith. It is as if we allow the soup to be poured over the bottom of our bowl while we skeptically refuse to turn the bowl right side up so as to receive enough to fill us spiritually. Many times we are able to fill our mind's computer with a great deal of factual or untrue knowledge, building, ever building the stockpile, increasing the self-image that we are an educated person, while we neglect any attempt to tap the vast reservoir of wisdom and truth to be found in the spiritual unknown. Once in awhile we wander into the infinity of spirituality, pushed possibly by catastrophy, thus adding a testimony to hug close to us without realizing that we could live in this beautiful place at all times if we held our faith high. When faith is, even in times of crisis, too weak to find the blessings of testimony, we turn to the arm of flesh, flesh usually as weak or weaker than our own, finding a cursing rather than a blessing. Some of us have a small shred of testimony bestowed upon us by parents or by the examples of bolder souls who have dared to find out. Having received this hope, we cling miserly to it, yet do we still fight against religion and God for fear we may prove the dreaded, haunting doubts we have secretly harbored to be true: "This is all there is, there is no more."

Still other times, having been conscience-stricken, we feel unworthy to ever receive such blessings of testimony, cowering from the out-stretched hand of God, refusing to accept the rich gifts He offers. We shrink into the shadows and say, to justify past sins, "I have already done wrong, a little more won't make any difference." We live so long with the same untried cliches and time-worn phrases of oft-quoted scriptures that we not only tire of their seeming old-fashionedness but refuse to give them a fair chance. We have heard the word "repentance" so often, and we associate it with so many things unpleasant, that we often lose the rewards of the joy and peace that are attached to the repentant moments. When by repentance we are snatched miraculously from precipices and placed again upon the solid road where God does not chastize us for the next time we may fall. He forgives us as of then, with the loving hope that we may remain on the solid road. Nature is more exacting in her laws and often seems less willing than God to grant forgiveness for sin; for when we eat poison, we die. Or when we are wounded severely, life can be over. Nature is still kinder than many suppose. The human body and soul can take a great deal more abuse, jumping back and forth from repentance to broken laws, than we realize before we must pay the uttermost final penalty. Some are able to get away with more abuse than others because of their inherent strength. Still, as soon as we begin to obey the laws upon which our bodies were created, we are rewarded almost immediately. All is not quite forgiven when irreversible damage has been done, but we do not have to wait for as long as it took us to arrive at a deplorable condition before health begins to improve. However, when God heals there can be a complete, immediate restoration to health of body and soul, with forgiveness for sin. There are people who have been recipients of new bones, people who have had internal organs changed or made new, a renewing of the body, a priceless gift for repentance. The part of these rewarding experiences that has probably done more to hinder inexperienced or fearful people from attempting to receive them is the smug, sanctimonious warblings of us who think we have an edge on the love of God because He has granted us a blessing during a moment of faithful repentance. We preach hellfire and damnation with all the assurance of one who thinks he has arrived, losing somewhere along the way the real loving, tender tolerance of Christ. The

215

first thing that happens to us with a little new-found knowledge is the loss of patience: "Why can't those around us see its benefits?" So we proceed in our critical way to try and straighten everyone out with the result that truth suffers many setbacks. Soaring high on the deceptive wings of self-righteousness, we cast a shadow, hindering the light of truth from descending on our fellowmen, placing ourselves as an obstacle in the way of someone's health or happiness.

Petrarch made an interesting observation in his comment to Clement VI:

"I know that your bedside is beleaguered by doctors, and naturally this fills me with fear. Their opinions are always conflicting, and he who has nothing new to say suffers the shame of limping behind the others. As Pliny said, in order to make the name for themselves through some novelty, they traffic with our lives. With them – not as with other trades – it is sufficient to be believed to the last word, and yet a physician's lie harbors more danger than any other. Only sweet hope causes us not to think of the situation. They learn their art at our expense, and even our death brings them experience; the physician alone has the right to kill with impunity. Oh, Most Gentle Father, look upon their band as an army of enemies. Remember the warning epitaph which an unfortunate man had inscribed on his tombstone: 'I died of too many physicians.'"

If man is to bring a millennium of one thousand years of peace and usher in the presence of Christ to rule and reign over him, he must be clean in mind, body, and spirit in order to endure the presence of Jesus Christ. We are told that at this time man will not taste of death; and in order to do this, he must have earned this translation by the things he has overcome in the flesh. Strange how we are always willing to sacrifice anything for health: a kidney, an eye, an arm, a leg, part of a stomach. We are even willing to place on the sacrificial altar of the operating table any part of our bodies, no matter what pain it may cuase us, in the hope of having health once more. But who of us is willing to sacrifice his appetite, not only the appetite for food but also sexual appetites. These are the most difficult sacrifices to make. The appetites of the flesh are the things we may have to overcome in order to be changed in the twinkling of an eye. When we achieve this cleanliness of soul and body, we will have no need of a physician, nor will be need the bitterness of herbal medicine.

The philosopher Herbert Spencer said,

"There is a principle which is – against all information, which is proof against all argument, and which can never fail to keep a man in everlasting ignorance. That principle is condemnation before investigation."

By the same token, let us not be so open-minded that everything that goes in falls out. There are some things in this world that are absolute: if we had not the ability to discern what they were, we would never have a testimony of anything. We have learned in our society that when we keep the outside of the body and our surroundings clean, we lessen the chances of disease on the surface of the skin; and we use a mouthwash to kill the germs as they enter the mouth, but we have not yet learned how to keep our bodies clean inside so that there is no food for the microbe. So we continue to fear, whenever anyone has a cold or a disease, that we might also be a victim. Disease cannot live in a body spiritually and physically clean and well nourished.

We have moved along since the time when Francis Bacon demanded experiments into a scientific industrial revolution; where science along with money has reigned as King; where research has lost itself in a maze of complex facts and figures always leaving the door open to new experimental results; thus allowing all new knowledge to remain for a time suspended in the air, until all the pieces have been put into place and all conclusions drawn. Often the wrong conclusions are then accepted as fact.

This has been an age of renaissance in all fields but the roots of decay are being observed. We have watched man learning many things of great value, and have seen him evolve through this period of free thinking from a dogmatic superstitious, prejudiced, war-like being, into a wishy-washy type who welcomes to believe everything but in reality believes little for sure, as modern sophistication allows few absolutes. We have watched the change from certain healthy, reassuring, spiritual convictions, while taking pride in an apathetic tolerance of religion, to a false concept of peace, which must be bought at all cost, even to the rejection of truth. Along with such apathy and moral decay, we are watching our renaissance fade into confusion and doubt.

As the drama of Earth life appears to be steadily progressing towards an epilogue, with prophecy being fulfilled on all sides, sanctification and purification of body and spirit will be the demands of the winding up the scenes, as the plagues, trials and tribulations of the last days spread over the Earth.

When we make the final change to a period of individual and collective revelation, learning by the spirit, while living in obedience, where God rules in the affairs of men, we will have run full circle to the millenium. In its glorious finality the world should not cause science to be consumed but rather in the interest of the world, enlarged upon and corrected, without the destructive forces we know today — when emotional presumptions are not the rule, nor uninformed prejudice. Pure revealed knowledge should change past fear to joy. Peace and real health could then follow. We see how then, "When man lives to the age of the tree, his food will be fruit."

BIBLIOGRAPHY

Allen, James. *As a Man Thinketh*.

Apocrypha, The. Tudor Publishing Co.

Asimov, Isaac. *The Chemicals of Life*. Signet.

Atkins, Robert C., M.D. *Dr. Atkins' Diet Revolution*. Mckay.

Bates, W. H., M.D. *Better Eyesight Without Glasses*. New York: Holt, Rinehart & Winston, Inc.

Bealle, Morris A. *Super Drug Story*. Columbia Publishing Co.

Beck. *Medicine in the American Colonies*.

Benard, Dr. R. "Herbal Elixirs of Life." Molelumn Hill, Cal.: Health Research.

Bhagavad Gita, The.

Blaine, Judge Tom R. *Mental Health Through Nutrition*. New York: Citadel Press

Brandt, Johanna. *The Grape Cure*. Catherines, Ontario: Provoker Press.

Bryan, Arthur H., Bryan, Charles A., Bryan, Charles C. *Bacteriology*. Barnes & Noble.

Burton, Jean. *Lydia Pinkham Is Her Name*.

Carque, Otto. *Vital Facts About Food*. Los Angeles: Kahan and Lessin Co.

Carson, Rachel. *Silent Spring*. Fawcett Publishing, Inc.

Carter, Mosley: *Microbiology and Pathology*.

Christopher, J.R. *Word of Wisdom*.

Christopher, J.R. *Herbal Lesssons*.

Clark, Linda. *Get Well Naturally*. The Devin-Adair Co.

Clough. *Diseases of the Blood*. Harper's Medical Monograph, Harper Brothers Publishing.

Cohen, A., Rev. *Everyman's Talmud*. E. P. Dutton & Co., Inc.

Cooley, Donald G. *Better Homes and Gardens Family Medical Guide*. Meredith Press.

Coon, Nelson. *Using Wayside Plants*. Hearthside Press, Inc.

Cooper, Kenneth H., M.D., M.P.H. *Aerobics*. Bantam Books, Inc.

Cuddon, Eric. *The Meaning and Practice of Hypnosis*. Citadel.

Culpepper, Nicholas. *Complete Herbal*. W. Foulsham & Co., Ltd.

Davis, Adelle. *Let's Eat Right to Keep Fit*. New American Library.

de Kruif, Paul. *The Male Hormone*. Garden City Publishing Co.

Dick-Read, Grantly, M.D. *Childbirth Without Fear*. Harper & Row, Pub.

Discourses of Brigham Young, arranged by John A. Widtsoe. Deseret Book Co.

Dunne, Desmond. *Yoga Made Easy*. Award Books.

Ehret, Arnold. *Roads to Health and Happiness*. Ehret Publishing Co.

Ehret, Arnold. *Rational Fasting*. Ehret Publishing Co.

Ehret, Arnold. *Mucusless Diet Healing System*. Beaumont, Cal.: Ehret Publishing Co.

Feasby, W. R., Hetenej, G., Jr., and Wrenshall, G. A. *The Story of Insulin*. Indiana Univ. Press.

Febiger, Goss and Lea. *Gray's Anatomy*.

Forbes, Allan W. *Our Friends the Bugs*. New York: Exposition Press.

Garrison. *An Introduction to the History of Medicine*. Philadelphia and London: W. B. Saunders Company.

Ghalioungui. *Magic and Medical Science in Ancient Egypt*.

Gibby, J. Melvin, *Sand for the Rails*. Deseret Book Co.

Haggard. *Devils, Drugs and Doctors*.

Hendrick, Ives., M.D. *Facts and Theories of Psychoanalysis*. Dell Pub. Co.

Hill, Napoleon. *Think and Grow Rich*. The Ralston Society.

Holmgren, Arthur H. and Andersen, Berniece A. *Weeds of Utah*. Special Report No. 21. Utah Agricultural Experiment Station, 1970.

Home Nursing Textbook. Nursing Services, American Red Cross. Doubleday, Inc.

Human Nutrition. U.S. Dept. of Agriculture, Report No.2, Aug. 1971.

Ingham, Eunice D. *Stories the Feet Have Told*. Published by author.

Jensen, Bernard, D.C., N.D. *The Science and Practice of Iridology*. Bernard Jensen Products Publishing Division.

Jensen, Bernard. Lectures. Solano Beach, Cal.: Bernard Jensen Products Publishing Co.

Johnson, Alan P. *Fasting the Second Step to Eternal Life*. Deseret Book Co.

Johnson, Carl M. *Common Nature Trees of Utah*. Special Report No.22.

Journal of Discourses.

Khan, Muhammad Zafrulla. *The Koran*. Arabic text, English translation. Praegar Publishers.

Kirschner, H. E., M.D. *Live Food Juices*. H. E. Kirschner Pub.

Kirschner, H. E., M.D. *Nature's Healing Grasses*. H. C. White Publications.

Kloss, Jethro. *Back to Eden*. Longview Publishing House.

Kneipp, Sebastian. *My Water Cure*. Jos. Koesel Publisher

Kreig, M. *Green Medicine*. Rand McNally.

Kriege, Theodor. *Fundamental Basis of Iris Diagnosis*.

Lander. *Walking in Obedience*. Bookcraft.

Levin, Meyer. *Classic Hassidic Tales Retold from Hebrew, Yiddish, and German Sources*. New York: Citadel Press.

Life and Works of Josephus, The. translated by William Whiston, New York: Holt, Rinehart & Winston.

Loeb, Carl. *The Black Out of Cooking*. Health Research.

Loewenfeld, Claire. *Herb Gardening*. Faber & Faber.

Lucas, Richard. *Nature's Medicines*. Parker Publishing Co., Inc.

Lundwall, N. B. *Assorted Gems of Priceless Value*. Bookcraft.

Luscher, Max. *The Luscher Color Test*. Random House, Inc.

Maimonides, Moses. *Treatise on Asthma*.

Maimonides, Moses. *Treatise on Poisons and Their Antidotes*.

Maimonides, Moses. *Treatise on Hemorrhoids*.

Maimonides, Moses. *The Guide to the Perplexed*. Dover.

Maltz, Maxwell. *Psycho-Cybernetics*. New York: Prentice-Hall, Inc.

Master Herbology. Research Technical Service.

McCoy, Frank. *The Fast Way to Health*. McCoy Publishing, Inc.

Meaning of the Glorious Koran, The. An explanatory translation by Mohammed Mormadukl Pickthal. The New American Library, the New English Library Limited.

Merck Manual of Diagnosis and Therapy, The. Merck, Sharp & Bohme Research Laboratories.

Meyer, Joseph E. *The Herbalist*. Rand McNally & Co.

Minken, Jacob S. *The World of Maimonides*. New York and London: Thomas Yoseloff, Publisher.

Moss. *Acupuncture and You*.

Muenscher, W. C. *Poisonous Plants of the U.S.*

Munn. *Psychology*. Houghton-Mifflin Co.

Public, Benedict Lust. *Your Kidneys Natural Method of Healing*. Natural Health Library.

Quigley, D. T. *The National Malnutrition*.

Rodale, J. L. and staff. *The Complete Book of Composting*. Rodale Books, Inc.

Rodale, J. L. *Organic Gardening*. Rodale Books, Inc.

Rodale, J. L. *The Prostate*. Rodale Press.

Rudolph, T. M., Ph. D. *Chlorophyll, Natures Green Magic*.

Sawitz, Wm., M.D. *Medical Parasitology*. Toronto: New York Blankiston Co.

Salter. *Conditioned Reflex Therapy*.

Schindler, John A., M.D. *How to Live 365 Days a Year*. Prentice-Hall, Inc.

Shute, Wilfrid. *Your Heart and Vitamin E*. Cardian Society Book Library.

Sinclair, Upton. *The Fasting Cure*. Published by the author.

Slaughter, Frank G., M.D. *Your Body and Your Mind*. Julian Messner, Inc.

Smith, Austin E. *Drug Research and Development*.

"Sun, Air and Light Baths." Mokelumne Hill, Cal.: Health Research.

Sweetland, Ben. *I Can*.

Szekely, Edmond Bordeaux. *The Essene Code of Life from the Orginal Aramic and French Translations*. San Diego: Academy of Creative Living.

Teachings of the Prophet Joseph Smith. Compiled by Joseph Fielding Smith. Deseret Book Co.

The Book of Mormon. Salt Lake City: Deseret Book Co.

The Doctrine & Covenants. Salt Lake City: Deseret Book Co.

The Holy Bible. Cleveland and New York: The World Publishing Company.

Tushnet, L., M.D. *The Medicine Man*. New York: Warner Paperback.

Tuttle, Schottelium, and Mosly. *Textbook of Physiology*.

Vishnudevananda, Swami. *The Complete Illustrated Book of Yoga*. New York: Julian Press, Inc., Publisher.

Walker. *The Story of Medicine*. New York: Oxford University Press.

Walker, N. W. *Become Younger*. Norwalk Press Publishers.

Walker N. W. *Raw Vegetable Juices*. Norwalk Press Publishers.

White, George Starr, M.D. *Zone Therapy*. Health Research.

World Book Encyclopedia.

Yogananda, Paramahansa. *Autobiography of a Yogi*. Self-Realization Fellowship.

222

223

NOTE: Headings in **BOLD CAPS** denote diseases and symptoms. **Bold page** numbers denote major treatment of subject.

224

225

226

225

226

Symptoms (cont.)

Cretinism - 155
Crying (involuntary) - 156
Cysts - 153
Dandruff - 142, 158
Dental care - 142, 149
Depression - 152, 153, 158, 160
Dermatitis - 145, 152
Diarrhea - 143, 146, 155, 157, 159
 Infant - 159
Digestive disorders - 160
Disc problems - 143, 149, 158, 164
Dizziness - 156, 160
Dropsy - 161
Drowsiness - 158
Ears - 144, 145, 163
Eczema - 145, 158
Edema - 149, 161
Epilepsy - 146
Exhaustion - 160
Eyelids swollen - 144
Eyes - 141, 146
Face puffy - 156
Fainting - 145
Fatigue - 101, 153, 155, 156, 161
Fear - 157-159
 of darkness - 154
Fingernails brittle - 156
Flu - 143
Gallstones - 142
Gas - 157
Gastritis - 143, 157, 160
Glands, swollen - 156, 160
Glaucoma - 160
Goiter - 155
Gout - 143, 149, 160
Growth retarded - 150
Gums swollen - 149, 150
Hair - 141, 152, 157, 164
Hallucinations - 152
Hands chapped - 154
Headache - 103, 160
Hearing dull - 156
 loss - 142
Heart disease - 155, 156, 161
Heat stroke - 163
Hemophilia - 152
Hemorrhages easy - 152
Hemorrhoids - 145
Hepatitis - 142, 149, 154
Hernia - 150

Hyperactivity - 157
Hypoglycemia - 160, 161
Impetigo - 142
Infection - 142
Insomnia - 153, 156, 157
Irradiation sickness - 149
Irritability - 153
Jaws - faulty development - 150
Joint disorders - 150, 155, 164
Kidney disorders - 146, 147, 154, 162, 167
Knee disorders - 143
Leg cramps - 153
 bowed - 150
Lethargy - 155
Listlessness - 161, 163
Ligaments - 161
Liver disorders - 142, 143, 154, 162, 164
Lumbago - 143
Memory impaired - 156, 159
Menstrual disorders - 146, 153, 164
Metabolic rate low - 143
Moodiness - 164
Motion sickness - 145
Mouth sore - 146
Muscle cramps - 145, 146, 149, 153, 157, 160
Muscle tone loss - 159, 161
Nails - 141
Nausea in pregnancy - 145
Nervous disorders - 143, 150, 153, 158, 160, 162, 163
Neuralgia - 143, 159
Neuritis - 145, 146
Nosebleed - 149
Numbness in limbs - 159
Ovaries swollen - 161
Pain - 153
Palpitations - 156, 157
Panic - 152
Paralysis - 143, 159, 161
Pigmentation during pregnancy - 149
Pregnancy cap - 155
 toxemia - 145
Psoriasis - 142, 145
Pulse weak - 155, 161
Pyorrhea - 149, 150
Sciatica - 143
Schizophrenia - 159
Sexual debility - 155, 164
Singing difficulty - 164

NOTE: Heading in **BOLD CAPS** denote diseases and symptoms. **Bold** page numbers denote major treatment of subject.